Gardening
in
the Minefield

Gardening in the Minefield

A SURVIVAL GUIDE FOR SCHOOL ADMINISTRATORS

Laurel Schmidt

HEINEMANN
Portsmouth, NH

Heinemann
A division of Reed Elsevier Inc.
361 Hanover Street
Portsmouth, NH 03801–3912
www.heinemann.com

Offices and agents throughout the world

Library of Congress Cataloging-in-Publication Data
Schmidt, Laurel J.
    Gardening in the minefield: a survival guide for school administrators /
by Laurel J. Schmidt.
        p. cm.
    ISBN 0-325-00476-5
    1. Elementary school principals—Handbooks, manuals, etc. I. Title.

LB2831.9 .S34 2002
372′.12′012—dc21

                                                                                        2002024344

Editor: Danny Miller
Cover design: Catherine Hawkes/Cat & Mouse Design
Author photo: Thalia King
Manufacturing: Louise Richardson

Printed in the United States of America on acid-free paper

06   05   04   03   02   DA   1   2   3   4   5

To my best mentors
John Shambra, Paul Heckman,
And, always, Durnford King

Contents

Acknowledgments

Good books, like good careers, are collaborative efforts. This is particularly so in the case of *Gardening in the Minefield*, a book that has been incubating in me for decades, though little did I know it. Since my entry into the teaching profession, I have enjoyed extraordinary friendships with passionate educators, most especially Pat Lem, Diana Donan, Susanne Henry, Anne Brown, Jason Roach, and Lisa Bartoli. I was fortunate to work with Edith Dury, Neil Schmidt, John Deasy, Pat Cairns, Sylvia Rousseau, Sue Toyryla, and Jane Murray.

I have been supported in all my endeavors, both teaching and writing, by a band of loyal friends—Karen Boiko, Bill Himelright, Viki Montera, Christina Cocek, and Marolyn Freedman. Special thanks to my brilliant editor, Danny Miller—all writers should have a Danny Miller at least once in their lives. And finally to my family—my courageous mother, Dorothy; my beloved father, Robert; my siblings, Sheryl, Bob, Richard, and David; my talented children, Thalia and Anthony; and my best friend and coach, my husband, Durnford King.

Introduction

I became a principal in spite of myself, after a scant twenty-three years in the classroom. Not exactly a meteoric rise, as careers go, but I had my reasons.

It's not that I hadn't been invited. Every few years a central office administrator would wander into my class, furrow his brow, and nudge my principal with a discreet inquiry. "Remind me again. Why's she still in the classroom?" as if a criminal past kept me from seeking a higher station in life. It's not that I was unqualified. I had an unused administrative credential in my sock drawer that was older than most middle schoolers.

The truth? I was willfully and persistently unimpressed with administration—it wasn't called Leadership in those days. I simply didn't get it. I watched my principal bound through the school, clearly passionate about his work. But what did he do all day? And more important, how could life that far from children have any meaning?

So I just kept learning about teaching. Every couple years I'd cajole my way into a new assignment, until finally I'd covered the waterfront, from kindergarten through middle school. I loved the chance to tackle a new curriculum, but mostly I just adored kids in any size, shape, or zip code. Finally, after decades of deeply satisfying work, I was lured from the classroom by an intelligent, progressive superintendent. He was looking for a new principal. I was looking for a new challenge. I had a lot to learn.

How hard was it to be a novice principal? Surprisingly, some parts of the job were so simple I could have sent in a body double. There were thousands of meetings, most of which hovered somewhere between plankton and krill on the food chain of life-changing events. The hardest part of the job was grappling with issues of social justice—racism, classism, and intolerance. The nod to equity and the thinly disguised scramble to be on the winning side of the gap. I was enraged by student support systems that were fine-tuned to the demands of a lawyer but stone-deaf to simple requests from poor families. I was hard on teachers who were hard on kids.

My performance was far from perfect. In fact, I fought for my share of the mistakes. Sometimes I took big risks. I locked horns with the staff and the community, touching off two or three spectacular pain festivals. Sometimes I blinked or cut my losses. I was a novice and I was scared. I had a lot to learn.

During the first year, my stress level went from Zen to stratospheric. I tried yoga breathing and a few unsuccessful trips to a masseuse, who pronounced in dismay, "You are veddy, veddy tense." I flunked massage, but I was a four-star, Olympic-gold teeth clencher. Each night I fell asleep with explicit instructions to myself—*Don't clench. Don't clench*—and routinely awoke to the sound of molar skating on molar.

You might say I wasn't a natural for the job.

Except that being a principal, if you do it right, is all about teaching and learning—the things I love most. It didn't take long to discover the work I was meant to do. I invested my energy in classrooms. Each week I questioned, coached, and carved out time to teach. I was awed by teachers, veteran and novice alike, so fierce in their dedication to learning, yet so gentle with the tender wonder of their students. I marveled at conversations between students in full discovery mode. Everywhere I turned there was growth—dozens of varieties of lush, vibrant growth. The school was a garden, and I the fortunate head gardener. I was supremely happy.

And the minefield?

Leading a school is highly public and political work. Hundreds, perhaps thousands, of young lives hang in the balance every day, and you are responsible. No matter how much you do, or how well you do it, you'll attract criticism, like iron filings to a magnet. You can do a hundred things right, but a single slip can quietly gnaw at you for weeks, or explode into a high-visibility disaster. There's no escaping it—if you choose to be a principal, the minefield is not optional.

But gardening is.

I discovered how to garden bit by bit—how to throttle the bureaucratic demands of the job into subservience so I could spend more time with kids, how to convey to my staff the urgency of our task, and celebrate the nobility of our collective exhaustion. On the best days, I was jubilant. On the toughest days, I consoled myself with the determined thought, "It's not failure—it's research." This book is a collection of what I gleaned and prodded from my experiences—in the garden and the minefield. It's one view of leadership—mine—and you may vigorously disagree with some of it, because leadership is an art, and there are many ways to do it well. But I hope it will help you master the practical challenges of the job, and learn to view your school as sacred ground where you till, plant, and harvest from one season to the next.

If you choose gardening, you'll need a clear idea of where you want to go and a deep and abiding belief that there are many ways to get there. Rent—but don't own—a thick skin to shield you from the generic brand of criticism that all principals attract—it comes with the territory. Train yourself to rejoice in the humanity and humor of daily life at school. Most important, stoke your passion for the art of teaching, and honor those who do it well.

Trust me. It's a garden out there, if you know where to step.

Gardening
in
the Minefield

1

Surveying the Terrain

Getting Smarter About the Politics of Education

- Bosses and Beneficiaries: Who's Who in the Politics of Education
- Why Johnny Still Can't Read: Current Views on Schooling
- Reform or Reconstitute: Solutions for Sale
- Thinking Politically: A Primer
- The Higher Road: Gardening in the Minefield

One rainy Saturday afternoon, in a last-ditch effort to avoid an overdue budget report, I decided to clean out my office closet, a jumble of hand-me-downs from a half-dozen former principals. It was like stumbling into the Smithsonian of education—complete with a tarnished silver tea set from bygone PTA gatherings, when ladies wore hats and gloves; boxes of yellowing budget reports, brittle as potato chips; purple ditto masters; tattered phonics kits, eager for a comeback; and a leather-bound photo album.

I opened the album and stared in quiet wonder at a 1940s version of myself. The principal sat, hands folded atop his desk, every inch of which was visible. Mine was a midden of mail and district memos. He looked composed and rested—I rarely slept beyond four-thirty, when anxiety woke me like a bugle. His face was untroubled by the complexity of shared decision making, and his communication needs were amply served by a single, shiny, black phone that took exactly one call at a time—no voice mail.

I wanted his job!

From Manager to Miracle Worker

Schools are deceptive-looking places. The sight of so many children conjures up memories of innocence, youthful energy, and hope. Casual observers imagine an enterprise fueled by dedicated adults earnestly fulfilling their philanthropic mission. If this were the case, school administration would be a sinecure, a rest cure, a picnic. It's not, and probably never was. But being a principal in the olden days certainly was easier—largely a matter of managing well-behaved women and their mostly docile charges, all done in a remote-controlly sort of way.

Then came the revolution. Sputnik exposed Americans as mathematically and scientifically challenged; *A Nation at Risk* gave America's schools a D plus; principals were catapulted out of their La-Z-Boys and into the role of change-agents. *School improvement* was the all-purpose mantra, and it was the principals' job to deliver. Their learning curve went vertical.

Since then, education has existed in a perpetual state of reform, and the role of the principal has been radically transformed. Schools have become complex learning communities, where governance groups the size of a small prairie town are encouraged to reach decisions on everything from budgets to textbooks. Even if it's been decades since the participants set foot inside a school, that distant experience as a student is credential enough to give them a significant voice in what the principal should—and shouldn't—do.

> *"Leaders are visionaries with a poorly developed sense of fear and no concept of the odds against them."*
>
> —Robert Jarvik

And what are twenty-first-century principals doing, sixty-plus hours per week? Attempting to revitalize schools so neglected that in fifty years there's been no change in the buildings, hallway linoleum, or trophy case—returning alumni can stroll down memory lane without the aid of their imaginations. Principals stretch shrinking budgets until they are paper-thin to finance mandatory federal programs, while cobbling together a patchwork of pro bono services to address the urgent social and emotional needs of their students. But most important, they are expected to galvanize their staffs into performing feats of instructional excellence that make their standardized test scores jump as if they've been electrocuted.

Satisfying all those expectations would be enough to bring full employment a small army of well-paid professionals. Instead, you—the Lone Principal—tackle the entire agenda with a skeleton crew and oceans of coffee. All the while, you're subject to a degree of scrutiny that would make a maximum-security warden proud. Like it or not, you perform every day in a highly political arena, observed and assessed by an array of "school watchers" ranging from federal and state agencies to the local merchants' association. They're deeply interested in your performance—though not necessarily your success—while you may have only the vaguest notion of their existence.

If you spent much time in the teaching ranks, it's unlikely that politics is your strong suit—many teachers are notoriously apolitical, and they like it that way. But as a school administrator, you can no longer afford to say, "I'm not into politics," because politicians are "into" you. Education is a hugely political, multi-trillion-dollar enterprise, and it takes more than a love of children and playground rules to survive.

So you need to get smarter about the political landscape of your job. This may seem like a relatively straightforward task—since all politics is local. But the politics of education is a tangle of relationships, agendas, money, and opportunity, with a vigorous but often covert life of its own. Understanding it could be a full-time job, but you already have one—leading a school—and even if you are determined to be "in the know," the view from your office— where you spend twelve to fifteen hours a day—is limited. By nightfall, you're probably too exhausted to drag yourself to school board meetings, or even plow through the two-hundred-page agenda. The actual appearance of board members at schools is running slightly behind Elvis sightings, and you'd have to be a human Richter scale to sense some decisions before they erupt in public, so developing your political savvy takes a bit of work. But it's worth it, because the politics of education can change your job radically, or leave you looking for a new one.

Bosses and Beneficiaries: Who's Who in the Politics of Educations

Few institutions touch so many Americans as closely as the public schools. Eager stakeholders range from senators and corporate heads to grandparents and crossing guards. They're spread across a vast ideological spectrum, from soaring idealism to profound pragmatism.

Education attracts big business and big power. While you and your staff are straining to close the achievement gap, many groups benefit politically or economically when schools fail—where you see low test scores, they see political capital or robust third-quarter profits. That's why it's called politics and not philanthropy.

The first rule of politics is *know the players*. Here's a short list of the groups shaping the politics of education, and setting the criteria by which your performance is judged. Keep your eye on them. They've got their eyes on you.

State and Federal Legislators

As our society lurches in one direction, or reverses course, legislators keep their finger to the wind and modulate their positions to meet the current demands. Schools are excellent barometers of public opinion, and provide ample material for campaign speeches. Once elected, legislators are at the top of the policy-making chart. Election rhetoric about improving schools is translated into laws, often with little input from a broad base of educators. As a principal, you're on the receiving end of policy. You bear the responsibility for compliance, even if it means rejecting best practices in favor of short-sighted, underfunded mandates.

Special-Interest Groups

The range of educational topics represented by special-interest groups covers the political spectrum: bilingual education, English-only, vouchers, charter and alternative schools, racial and ethnic issues, gay and lesbian education, prayer in schools, special education, pro-tests and anti-tests. Special-interest groups exert pressure through political action committees and huge campaign donations, skillfully engaging the press to amplify their ideological wars. They finance slates of candidates for school board offices, often radically changing the direction of an entire district, including curriculum, assessment, and expectations for you and your staff.

Taxpayers

In some cities, up to 85 percent of the residents have no children in school, but they vote for or veto local taxes for schools. So they want to know, What's the district spending their money on? Without a direct link to the schools, they may rely on their neighbors or the local press to gauge how well you're doing. If the headlines trumpet frequent drug busts and strike-prone employee groups, voters doubt that they're getting their money's worth. The resulting drop in revenues perpetuates a vicious cycle of crumbling buildings, low salaries, and insufficient materials. In many districts, principals are expected to be public-relations machines by day, and to organize get-out-the-vote phone banks by night.

The Media

The media have a profound impact on state and national policy. In large measure, they determine the way education is viewed by government, business, and the public. Unfortunately, good school news is usually consigned to the obligatory community column, while bad news—shootings, plummeting test scores, mismanagement—is above the fold. Local school boards are usually covered by cub reporters with little understanding of local history or complex educational issues. Some resort to negative, sensational reporting that may create the appearance of controversy, and alarm the public. Having made their mark, they move on to bigger assignments, while principals deal with the residual questions, backlash, and distrust in the community. Many good leaders—principals and superintendents—have fled their jobs to escape this harassment.

Private Enterprise

Failing schools are a lucrative target for entrepreneurs who promise to deliver better education, in better facilities, on a smaller budget—and reward investors. Privatization of public schools means that public funds are rerouted to for-profit school management companies, such as Edison Schools Inc. This radical solution continues to snag headlines and offer an apparent alternative when desperate school districts reach strike two in a three-strikes world. The New York City–based Edison currently manages 136 schools in twenty-three states, but has yet to produce significant changes in student achievement.

Big Business

Bad schools can also be good for big business, especially those that publish and distribute standardized tests, test preparation materials, data processing services, and textbooks. Low-performing schools fuel the gravy train for consultants, lobbyists, research institutes, and a host of other businesses that cater to educational forecasters and fix-it men. CEOs from very big business are invited to education summits to set policy, although there's little indication that these meetings amount to more than networking opportunities with phonics and Bloom's taxonomy on the menu.

The Local Business Community

Good schools are profit magnets for local business. The chamber of commerce, Rotary, and especially the real estate board all depend on the reputation of their city schools for their prosperity. Higher test scores mean higher real estate prices. Affluent families support a host of retail enterprises. So negative media coverage or falling test scores can reverberate throughout the local economy. The business community protects its vested interest in education through generous campaign contributions for business-friendly board members and direct financial support to schools that boost their city's reputation as the place to raise kids.

The Board of Education

School board members are local residents who worked hard to get elected. Some are starting a political career that may end in Washington, D.C., while others will serve their community schools for decades. It's a difficult job, and reelection depends on the perception that they are running good schools, including yours.

Board members are attuned to parents, business, and the press. If they're plagued with emails from worried citizens and merchants because your test scores appear to be wearing cement shoes, or drug pipes are more plentiful than calculators on campus, they must take action or forfeit their right to lead, so you will feel the heat.

Your Superintendent

Talk about a short shelf life! The average residency for superintendents is just over three years. They serve at the pleasure of the board, which means when elections create a whole new board, or ideology shifts, the superintendent may end up choosing between his beliefs and a paycheck.

To survive, some superintendents reverse course, sending mixed messages to the principals, or no signals at all. Others simply resign, so there's a new sheriff in town every few years. If the latest arrival pulls whole-school reform out of his bag of tricks and insists on a single, regimented approach to instruction, you're the one who has to make it work with your staff. Your credibility as an instructional leader is on the line, along with your job. This is when politics can go from local to loco, and it's no fun at all.

The Parents

Parents are voters and taxpayers. Their satisfaction with schools—your school—keeps board members in office and local dollars flowing into school coffers, so their opinions really matter. Surveys show that they want safe schools with high standards and competent teachers. Beyond that, most of them have no interest in the minutia of your school. They just want to feel confident that kids are at the top of everyone's agenda, and that your daily goal is always the same—helping kids achieve their full potential—whatever it takes.

Your district also has a core of watchdog parents who have attended every school board meeting for the last decade. They contribute to campaigns, lead the charge on bond issues, and may even function as a shadow cabinet for the superintendent. They have a huge vested interest in the schools, and a lot of clout.

When they're unhappy, these parents may skip the recommended conversation with you, and complain directly to the superintendent or a board member. The temperature at work can rise significantly, or become arctic, depending on how your supervisor deals with public discontent. On the flip side, parents can decide that you're just what the doctor ordered for their school and inform the district that hiring you was near genius. Having your own personal cheering squad may sound great, but problems arise if their enthusiasm stems from frustration with your staff or the hope that you'll solve problems that have vexed the school for years. They may expect major changes, even firings, shortly after you arrive. Siding with these parents can earn you enemy status with your own staff. If you publicly support the staff, parents may write you off as just another bureaucrat.

School-Site Governance Groups

Many districts have adopted a form of shared decision making that creates governance groups at each school site, composed of staff, parents, community, and administrators. Governance groups often control large parts of the school budget, and have subcommittees that work on curriculum, hiring, and school improvement. Principals charged with steering governance work must know how to focus the efforts of diverse interest groups, build trust and support for a single school vision, manage conflict, prioritize important issues, and coach stakeholders toward mastery of collaborative decision making. In some cases, it would be easier to start your own country. Keep your mentor on speed-dial if you're new to management-by-governance.

The Teachers' Union

While teachers as individuals are largely apolitical, their unions are not. Originally formed to protect teachers from unfair administrators and fight for decent salaries, unions also weigh in on issues such as vouchers, standards, and teacher evaluation. Yet they've been notably quiet on high-stakes testing, despite the punitive consequences for teachers in underperforming schools. Apparently, they view accountability testing as the lesser of two evils—the greater being the rise of for-profit schools that promise to improve education using nonunion teachers.

Unions in the Teacher Union Reform Network (TURN) project are determined to take the lead in building high-performing schools that provide better learning and higher achievement for all students. They vigorously embrace their responsibility for maintaining a high-caliber teacher corps through professional development and improve instuction by coaching and monitoring the effectiveness of their teachers.

Your local union representatives attend every board meeting, comment on many of the agenda items, and always have a quote ready for the press. If there are issues brewing at your school, you may make headlines or at least earn a few unflattering paragraphs in the union newsletter.

Teachers

Most teachers are remarkable adults whose remembrance of childhood is still fresh enough that they can travel each day into the world of young people, and lure them into the world of learning. For this they are generally underpaid and undervalued. Yet teachers are the only people who can ensure educational success. If it's not happening in a classroom, it's not happening, and no amount of "teacher-proof" curriculum can change that.

Teachers make education work, yet they're so removed from the politicians and decision makers that they might as well be manning a classroom in another galaxy. Many of them vigorously eschew all things political, as if avoiding a bad smell, and in return, politicans and researchers ignore teachers, which is why they're rarely included in the highest levels of reform work. In fact, teachers are often the last to know.

There will be the occasional power struggle between teachers and administration at a school site, usually led by a union representative. Truly unhappy teachers will often forge bonds directly with politically connected parents to resist reform or oust an unpopular administrator. It looks political, but much of the action is simply self-preservation.

From this roster it should be fairly clear that public schools are highly political and potentially turbulent environments. Everyone has an opinion about how you should do your job, while few regard your work with children as an attractive career choice.

Why Johnny Still Can't Read: Current Views on Schooling

With all those stakeholders weighing in on the state of the schools, you might expect opinions to be fairly diverse. In fact, the predominant message about education is persistently grim. Headlines insist that schools are failing, and the scramble to reform them would seem to indicate that somebody powerful is reading those shrill stories—or writing them. Here are some common views portrayed in the media.

- There was a golden age of education, when all students attended safe neighborhood schools, met rigorous standards, and graduated. Now America's schools are falling apart, thanks in part to top-heavy bureaucracies and ineffective administrators.
- The trillions of dollars spent on propping up education in the past generation were wasted. Underperforming schools were actually rewarded because low scores qualified them for special funding.
- Principals don't know how to improve failing schools. It's time to give other people a crack at it.
- Underprivileged students are trapped in failing schools because their parents are denied the right to choose government-financed alternatives.
- American students cannot compete in a global economy with a provincial education. We have lost our edge.

On the other hand, there is the tale of the fiercely ignored Sandia report, published in 1991 by the Sandia National Laboratories and released to exactly no fanfare in 1993. It reported that the state of education in the United States was far less gloomy than the public was being led to believe. Specifically, the findings stated that: high school completion rates and college graduation rates were the highest in history; one in four Americans has at least a bachelor's degree—the highest percentage in the world; a larger percentage of twenty-two-year-olds in the United States hold degrees in math, science, or engineering than in any of the nation's major economic competitors; far more students are taking Advanced Placement exams; and more teachers are subject to rigorous standards for certification and promotion today than in the past.

> *"Never doubt that a small group of thoughtful, committed people can change the world. Indeed, it is the only thing that ever has."*
>
> —Margaret Mead

The explanation for the Sandia report's nonappearance in the press? Think politically, just for a minute. Ask yourself, Who would benefit from this good news? Not the people demanding more money for schools, nor those stumping for vouchers or privatization as the only way to save us from becoming a nation of diploma-toting illiterates. The moral: sometimes good news is no news.

Here's another interesting bit of data that is much closer to home for most principals. Surveys consistently show that 70 percent of parents report being pleased with the education that their kids are getting in public schools, while only 40 percent believe that schools overall are doing a good job. Personal experience tells them that schools work, while the media says it isn't so.

This is not to say that all is well in our schools, but simply to assert that many schools are doing excellent work in the face of significant challenges; that intelligent, talented staffs led by courageous leaders are irrevocably changing the lives of children for the better; that at its heart, education is still an enterprise fueled by a passion for learning that survives the most stifling reforms.

Reform or Reconstitute: Solutions for Sale

Every school district seems to be in the market for a cure to what apparently ails education, with different groups proposing wildly different solutions, often in brutal public clashes. As a principal, you're acutely aware that kids will be the losers if you fall flat on your face, but do you realize that there will also be winners? Educational companies, special-interest groups, and politicians will take your failure and run with it, touting their solutions, with no guarantee that students will be any better served. The scale of the current reform effort is Herculean. The results? Just keep your ears open for the sound of a pendulum whooshing by.

Here's a menu of current remedies being proposed, implemented, or in some cases, prematurely debunked and consigned to the dustbin.

- national education standards
- whole-school reform
- tightly defined, proven curriculum
- rigorous standardized tests
- reconstituting failing schools
- increased teacher training
- vouchers, charter schools
- for-profit schools
- homeschooling

What does the man on the street propose as a remedy? Most Americans say that the government spends too little on education, and that the lack of funding contributes to problems in education, but when questioned about raising local taxes to support school improvement, business leaders and parents seem to agree in large numbers that student achievement can be lifted by ensuring safe schools with qualified teachers, rather than by raising per-pupil spending.

The frustration for principals is that most of the people engaged in the battle to reform schools are virtual warriors. They chair meetings, draft legislation, take votes, write complicated business plans or generous checks, but then they go off to their other lives. Board members return to their day jobs, provocative reporters and nimble legislators move on to hotter topics. Only principals and teachers show up at school every day and try to make the system work for kids, despite all its legitimate flaws and self-serving detractors.

Thinking Politically: A Primer

There's very little you can do to stop some political trends from barreling down on your school, faster than a speeding locomotive, even if you're a Superprincipal. But you can learn to think politically, if only to shed light on some of those puzzling out-of-the-blue decisions that make you want to blurt out, *Why would they do that?* earning yourself a round of furtive glances that confirm your status as either an outsider or naïve.

To think like a politician, you'll need to be part mathematician, part analyst, and part skeptic, with the observation skills of a social scientist. Don't take things at face value. Develop the habit of asking good questions. When faced with a puzzling situation or a complex and sensitive decision, interrogate yourself with the zeal of an IRS agent on commission. Start by asking:

- Who would benefit from this? Politically? Economically?
- Who would be opposed? Why?
- What would bring the two sides closer together?
- Are there unintended consequences that are beneficial? Detrimental?
- Who else will stand up for this? Why? Why not?

Then go the politicians one better. Ask the ethical questions:

- What effect does this have on kids?
- Do kids deserve this, even if it makes my life harder?
- Am I up for the fight?
- Is this a good use of my time?

There are other ways to develop your political antennae. Cruise your district website for announcements, letters from the superintendent, and policy updates. Read the agendas of school board and city council meetings.

They're posted in public and usually available online. Learn about district politics by participating in strategic planning activities or serving on hiring committees. Attend candidates' forums before elections and listen between the lines. Follow the local press coverage of education, especially the editorials and letters to the editor. Ask if your chamber of commerce has an education subcommittee and drop in on their meetings. Grab a front-row seat at board meetings, or climb into bed with a snack and follow the proceedings on your local cable station. You never know when you'll learn something that will save your job.

The Higher Road: Gardening in the Minefield

Survival is important, but it's hard to convince yourself that you're having a full and satisfying career simply because you arrive home each night with a full set of limbs. There's more to leadership than that.

There's gardening.

Gardening is delicate, complicated work composed of countless individual, interlocked triumphs and discoveries. It takes patience tempered with flashes of fervor about the urgency of lost opportunities. To be effective, it needs to stir questions, discussion, even arguments. So if you really want to lead a school, expect to think, though not necessarily easy thoughts.

Gardening is painfully this-worldly—the grueling schedule, the political uncertainties, the lifesaving nature of the work itself. And at the same time it is other-worldly—the other world being that of children, who have yet to experience life as we know it. Gardening gives you a steady focus in a world of shifting power and priorities, and transforms the exhausting, tenuous job of school leadership into a noble calling.

> *"In the struggle for justice, the only reward is to participate in the struggle."*
> —Stephen Douglas

2
The Vision Thing

Getting Smarter About Charting Your Course

- The Quest: Identifying Your Vision
- The Trick of It: Transplanting the Vision
- Night Vision: Parents as Partners
- In Living Color: Vision and Action

"The first thing you should do is some visioning!" I stared at the assistant superintendent's lips, and commanded my face to convey an eager "tell me more." Meanwhile, my mind froze. After a decade of parochial school, *visioning* was about as grammatically attractive as an electrified fence.

That said, you won't be surprised to learn that I never did a formal "visioning" process with my community. I was handed a vision statement when I arrived, and for the life of me, I couldn't imagine why it had taken six months of community wrangling to produce it. When the committee asked if I thought anything was missing, I vigorously suppressed, "A white cane with a red tip?" We couldn't find our way to the playground with that document, much less to a place where underachieving students were performing at levels similar to their high-scoring peers. What passed for a vision statement was simply a proxy for the status quo.

But I didn't lose any sleep over it because I had a vision of my own. And since I was the one chosen by the community to lead the school, I thought that counted for something. So I decided to try the show-and-tell approach to "visioning." I just started a conversation about teaching and learning. I talked to small groups and large, and insisted that they talk back. I wrote. I dragged people through classrooms with lists of questions to guide their interactions with students. I lured staff into examining student work and cajoled parents into taking standardized tests—which they enjoyed

13

about as much as their kids do, but argued more over who had the right answer!

Six or seven times a month, parents, educational experts, professors, staff, and I grappled with what it means to learn. I became a human sandwich board for my all-kids agenda. It was exhausting and exhilarating—and the only way I could imagine we would arrive at an understanding about what we, the adults, should be doing with students.

You may be thinking, "I know I have a vision, and if I had ten uninterrupted minutes, I could probably think up a dynamite statement." This chapter can help you jump-start the process.

The Quest: Identifying Your Vision

Most principals are like me. They go into administration because they have a passionate notion about how schools should work, and they're willing to road test their ideas in public. Their vision may be a collection of things that have worked or the product of a doctoral dissertation. It may be research based or emanate from deep in the gut. Whatever the origin, it drives them, and with the right skills, it can guide an entire educational enterprise.

I know there's been great emphasis in school leadership circles on the co-construction of a vision, with the principal facilitating the process. There are dozens of books that can teach you how to do that. This isn't one of them. I want you to think about *your* vision because I truly believe that communities choose leaders, fully expecting a vision as part of the package. And more important, if you don't have your own vision, how will you know if you're heading in the right direction? How will you know when you've arrived?

So, what's your vision? Identifying it isn't nearly as metaphysical as it sounds. A vision is a clear statement of every child's educational birthright, communicated through focused action. Another way to think about it is, "If nothing else, what will I guarantee all students who come to my school?"

You can zero in on your vision statement in one week if you're willing to observe yourself. Pay attention to what you do and what you say. Then answer these questions.

1. What do I plan for?
2. What do I model?
3. What do I assess?
4. What do I reinforce through recognition and celebration?

5. What behavior am I willing to confront?

6. What's worth a trip to the barricades?

Ask a few colleagues to answer the same questions about you, from their point of view. Take all that information, analyze it, and you should see a pattern of behavior that is vision driven.

> *"Don't be afraid to take a big step if one is indicated. You can't cross a chasm in two small jumps."*
> —David Lloyd George

Embedded in the very notion of a vision is the ability to see something that's not readily apparent, or doesn't even exist. So your vision should be a picture of possibilities, a reach into a better future. In every case, kids must be the beneficiaries. Here are some themes that may be at the heart of your vision:

equal access to quality instruction

social justice

clear expectations

service learning

parents as partners

early intervention

instructional excellence

authentic assessment

differentiated instruction

academic rigor

mainstreaming and inclusion

nurturing the whole child

the community as classroom

All too often, school leaders talk about one set of beliefs—their vision—but devote their energy to completely different issues. I knew a principal who touted "time on task" as the key to student success, but never had time to observe classroom tasks because he was too busy shadowing the custodians. Another school promised academic rigor for all students, then slashed the number of honors classes because their low student-teacher ratio made them too expensive. The motto Success for All was adopted by the same staff that doubled the number of referrals to special education because general education teachers had not been trained to make the accommodations that many kids need to succeed.

> *"Nothing contributes so much to tranquilize the mind as a steady purpose—a point on which the soul may fix its intellectual eye."*
>
> —Mary Wollstonecraft Shelley

Staff and community will decide what's truly important to you by noticing where you focus. If you want your words and actions to match, use your vision as the criteria by which you identify the essentials and prioritize your work, so you can channel your limited time and energy into achieving those pictures of possibility. With every new task you undertake, ask yourself, Will this get us closer to the vision?

The Trick of It: Transplanting the Vision

Now the trick is to transfer the vision from your head into the teachers' hands—literally—to infuse your passion into their actions so they become the primary agents of the educational birthright.

How does that happen? You can't use ventriloquism, hypnotism, sleight-of-hand, or any educational jiggery-pokery if you want authentic change. The trick is simply to notice. Notice approximations of what you want. Then make a big, big deal out of them. Do that consistently, with relentless enthusiasm, and the vision begins to take hold.

Teachers do this all the time. They start the year with goals and plans for where they want their classes to be in June. Then the kids walk through the door the first day, and there are at least a hundred things wrong with them. They're noisy, they can't write, they have no interest in school. Smart teachers don't say a word. Instead, they prospect for an approximation of the behavior they want and pounce on it—praising, thanking, and reinforcing this phantom of their vision. Pretty soon, the behavior multiplies. More praise from the teacher. And so it goes.

The same approach works with your staff. Search for approximations of your vision. Check in the chemistry lab, on the soccer field, in a drama class, or kindergarten. Whenever you uncover tangible evidence of your vision, trumpet your discovery to staff and parents. Shower the "doer" with genuine interest and recognition. That creates curiosity among the staff, if only of the what's-she-raving-about-now variety. But that's a start. Broadcast more vision pictures, and as you describe your findings, explain why they are important to kids.

I watched four students design, test, and redesign a paper airplane today. While they worked, they used terms like lift, drag, energy, and balance in scientifically precise ways. They weren't doing science, they were working as scientists.

Today Ms. Sloane's chemistry students staged a debate on whether our city council should fluoridate the town's water. Half the class argued using Internet research data, the other half used reasons collected in a survey from city voters. They were shocked to discover the power of emotions over science. One group decided to go speak to the city council. Thank you, Ms. Sloane, for helping your students discover the impact of chemistry on our daily lives. Good luck at the meeting.

The harder you look, the more approximations of your vision you will find. If you make them the centerpiece of every professional conversation, they will proliferate. It's a matter of time and persistence—but it beats shadowing the custodian.

Finding evidence of your vision in anecdotes around campus sets you up for success. Instead of importing some ivory-tower theory and hoping the staff will "get religion," you're touting a homegrown product, with your teachers as the source. You silence the naysayers who claim, "That would never work here," because it's already working, among their own colleagues and students. Most important, it sends a message about what's right with your school, avoiding the taint of criticism that accompanies so many reform movements. In effect you're saying, "I like what I see. How can we do even more?"

This approach is a huge relief to teachers who have spent entire careers cast in the role of lab rats for the latest educational experiments. Some won't follow through on any new idea because they believe it will just be replaced by another, and another, and another. Their capacity for responding to reform has dimmed to the point of nonexistence. But if you find the good in what they're already doing, you're over the first big hurdle.

Supporting Curiosity About Your Vision

As principal you have the power to start and sustain a conversation that always ends in the same place. What is a child's educational birthright? Are we delivering for all kids or just the eager and talented? You need to talk about your vision often and enthusiastically. Use vivid imagery and lots of anecdotes from your travels around the school. But talk is not enough. Demonstrate. Show and tell. Give staff time and opportunities to observe, ask questions, and experiment with your ideas in complete safety. Encourage experiments, and celebrate successes and failures as evidence of growth and opportunities to get smarter. And above all, remain steadfast in the face of the inevitable problems.

That's how a vision becomes a game plan and eventually—if you live long enough—a school culture.

You'll need to be supportive and explicit with staff. When you're visiting classes and see approximations of your vision, tell teachers precisely what they did that is "visionary." Quote their own words back to them to make your point. For example, "When your students asked you a question about the cause of the Boston Tea Party, you remarked about what a good question it was and then you asked the whole class to speculate on the answer. You are using inquiry techniques very effectively."

Ask teachers to describe the most effective ways that they could learn more about your vision and describe the ways you will support their learning. Since I was busy harvesting samples of my vision from every corner of the campus, it was logical that teachers could profit from watching each other, so Tuesday became peer-visiting day. I taught one class from nine to ten. My assistant principal took another from ten to eleven. That released two teachers to observe peers and ask questions. Veterans and novices took advantage, and I loved my time back in the classroom. I also organized brown-bag seminars for lunchtime, so teachers could eat and listen to a guest lecture on occupational therapy or environmental science. When the demand for information on autism swelled, I offered dinner at my house, so we could have a block of uninterrupted time to really dig into the topic and a tasty meal.

You gain credibility when you say something is important to you, and two months later it still is. You gain credibility and respect when you consider your teachers' needs as learners and provide a variety of opportunities for everyone to get smarter.

Night Vision: Parents as Partners

Just when you think you can't handle another responsibility, someone mentions the parents. They are the major stockholders in your educational enterprise, with deeply personal reasons to support your efforts to deliver the educational birthright to their kids. That's assuming that they understand your vision. If you don't take time to explain your vision to parents, over and over again, you could find your effectiveness being measured with criteria that belong in the Don't column of a best-practices manual. Here's why.

In any parent population there will be people with strong opinions about how you should run your school. Parents who were star students and who graduated to successful adult lives expect you to replicate their school experience for their kids. Others hated school and are willing to bet that things haven't changed much. The first time their child comes home complaining, you get branded with the same iron as their nemesis from years ago. Many parents think that you're only as good as your test scores—you don't need a vision if you can use a calculator. Finally, there's a large group of if-it-was-good-enoughers—people who found school boring and irrelevant, but can't see why you should get yourself or the community all in a lather just to make learning more interesting for their kids; it's good enough. What you have is a case of dueling visions.

Educating parents about your vision is time-consuming, retail work. Much of it takes place after dinner when you'd just as soon be at home, in your pajamas, heading for a good book. But not educating parents about your vision is a giant land mine with your name on it. A handful of underinformed parents have been known to derail entire math programs for at-risk students simply because it didn't "look" like the algebra they had in high school.

The challenge, of course, is that your parent group is as diverse as your student body. They have different degrees of prior knowledge, different learning styles, different social and emotional needs that affect their relationship with you. You may find yourself in a community where a handful of people have been the keepers of the vision for so long that many parents have given up and wandered off, concluding that school works for some kids, but not theirs.

If you're going to reach all of them, remember that one size doesn't fit all. You will need to offer your vision around the clock, in writing and in person, with and without visual aides. Orchestrating a parent-education program is a lot of work, but a very powerful way to multiply learning opportunities for kids. Here are some of the ways you can serve up little pieces of your vision to a broad spectrum of parent learners.

- Have morning coffees once a week. Set up a coffeepot in a comfortable room and meet with any parent that drops by.
- Schedule guest speakers, including therapists, child or adolescent psychologists, college recruiters, SAT prep specialists, educational therapists, speech pathologists, medical professionals, brain researchers, substance abuse counselors, law enforcement representatives, and emergency preparedness experts.
- Set up a lending library of parent-friendly books, audiotapes, and videotapes on educational topics.
- Sponsor family math and family science nights.
- Establish parent discussion/support groups that meet monthly to delve into a specific topic such as learning disabilities, early childhood development, parenting teens, bilingual education, or support for minority students and parents.

- Publish a weekly or monthly newsletter that features at least one article by you devoted to the children's educational birthright and how all adults can help attain it. Be sure your newsletter is translated for language groups other than English.

- Set up a monthly inquiry group for parents to deal with hot topics like standards, testing, exit exams, zero-tolerance, textbook adoptions, changes in board policies, and the latest theories on how kids learn.

- Organize a school volunteer course, in which you teach volunteers about best practices for working with students before they go into classrooms.

- Have a monthly walk-through for parents and community members so they can see your vision in the flesh. Start with a warm-up session where you present your vision of learning, do a question-and-answer segment, and then give parents a list of things to look for in each environment. You can use a version of the checklists found in Chapter 8. Have volunteers take small groups through selected classrooms. If you want to give feedback to the staff, have visitors fill out a response card before leaving.

> *"To accomplish great things, we must dream as well as act."*
> —Anatole France

In Living Color: Vision and Action

A great vision is pure potential. If you truly want parents and staff to understand and ultimately live your vision, they'll need a series of authentic experiences over time. There are thousands of effective ways to bring a vision to life. Here are some activities that you might see if the principal's vision were: *We are a community of learners.*

- Give kindergartners or incoming freshmen welcome letters from the principal describing learning at the school.

- Announce assemblies so parents and relatives can come and learn alongside their kids.

- Use community scientists as coaches and mentors for the science fair.

- Offer vigorous parent-education programs on a variety of topics, including parenting techniques, homework without tears, coping with ADHD, family literacy activities, and multiple intelligence theory.

- Organize support/discussion groups for specialty topics—special education, transition, parenting adolescents, how to choose a college, gifted programs.
- Hold brown-bag seminars for teachers at lunchtime.
- Organize book shares—free books donated, traded, and reused.
- Publish a list of learning opportunities in the surrounding community.
- Publicize staff development by having teachers write a summary of what they learned, to put in the parent newsletter column, "We Are All Learners."
- Sponsor family math or science nights.
- Sponsor quilt shows, hobby day, or family history day, and bring in parents and grandparents as teachers.
- Sponsor an intergenerational art show—students, parents, and grandparents all in one exhibit.
- Invite local authors to do a reading and book signing.
- Devote part of each PTA meeting to showing student work.
- Start every parent meeting with a teacher talking about or demonstrating learning in his class.
- Feature at least one article about learning in your newsletter. The Internet is loaded with short articles your can copy, quote, or excerpt.
- Post student work of all kinds throughout school with captions and quotes from the students annotating the work.

Double Vision

Although the idea of a vision for your school sounds ephemeral, in reality it's one of the most concrete applications of leadership. You see your vision in the lunch line, on the playfields, and on the auditorium stage. You can photograph, videotape, and document a myriad of activities that testify to its presence. When vision-driven interactions and events become commonplace in your school, go back to your office, put your feet up on your desk, and dream harder. Your vision is the future of your school.

3
Principal Dearest
Getting Smarter About Cutting the Cord

- Unparenting the Unglued: Reframing Personnel Crises
- Enabling: Eight Steps to Effective Problem Solving
- Other Office Visits: Strategies for Chronic Cases
- Rethinking Entitlement

Late one afternoon, when I had a clear shot at answering all my email before dark, two heads popped in my door, seeking an impromptu conference. I recall that I was starving—would have killed for a Big Mac or a big anything. Instead, I was staring at two faces wearing don't-hate-me grins, and fantasizing about eating French fries. I never even eat French fries.

Their mission was admirable—to make me a better principal. I think my silence suggested that their crash course wasn't going well, so as a parting gesture, they offered me an analogy, wrapped in a Norman Rockwell painting. It began innocently enough. "In a family," observed the designated hitter, "the father takes care of the mother, and the mother takes care of the baby." My jaw was gaping visibly at this point, but she plunged heedlessly on. "In school, the principal takes care of the teachers, so they can take care of the kids." I was tempted to blurt out, "Who takes care of the father?" but held my tongue. Instead, I hoisted my face up into a smile, and felt my stomach turn. My appetite had vanished.

This exchange was mind-boggling, until I remembered that my best friends and I called our favorite principal "Father." We adored him, were frustrated by him, and followed him from one town to another to enjoy his benevolent leadership.

A Family Affair

Shortly after that visit, I had a chat with a gifted psychiatrist, Dr. Daniel Siegel, who had been the director of the psychiatric intern program at the university.

22

He explained that in any organization, the leader assumes a parental role in the subconscious of the followers. Their unresolved child-parent issues, or fantasies about how life would have been with the perfect mom or dad, are awakened in principal-employee interactions, especially if you are the new boss on the block. *Will she notice me? What if he likes some staff more than others? Can I be honest, or will she need stroking?*

I mulled it over, and decided that this unconscious family idea made a lot of sense, especially when you consider that from the colonial period until the late twentieth century, America's schools were run by men; women were grateful just to sneak into the lowest ranks of one of the few professions that would have them. As recently as 1987, only 2 percent of all principals were women. That's up to 35 percent today, but men still account for 96 percent of school superintendents. All things considered, education as an institution still looks a lot like the traditional family. That Norman Rockwell analogy was right on the money: the principal *is* the dad—or mom.

The Principal Is In

Some principals actually enjoy this parental role, liberally distributing Kleenex and advice. Some even try their hand at homegrown psychology, imagining that if they establish a supportive relationship—lo, a miracle—the dysfunctional teacher will be inspired enough to plan adequate lessons, and even show up at work more than three days out of five. But personalities don't change, and some people are simply wedded to their discontent, so your efforts to increase their mental health quotient are seeds scattered on stone. Even if they seem momentarily receptive, backsliding is inevitable and you end up feeling like Sisyphus, Incorporated.

Plus, principal-therapists get burned. If the struggling teacher doesn't respond to your interventions, you may find yourself in the awkward role of failed therapist and reluctant evaluator. You could also face some uncomfortable questions from the union representative defending the employee. "You say you have concerns about her mental health, yet you trust her with children? Did you ever put your concerns in writing? Do you have a list of the suggestions and support you provided? Did you refer this teacher to counseling? Why not?" It goes straight downhill from there.

> *"Leaders must be close enough to relate to others, but far enough ahead to motivate them."*
>
> —John Maxwel

On the other hand, you don't want to bar your door, because it's equally dangerous to neglect personal relations. Poor interpersonal skills are the number-one reason why principals are fired. Distant, brusque, or insincere school leaders simply don't last, no matter how much they know about budget or assessment. Effective principals learn to use positive professional strategies to assist their staff in crisis and boost productivity.

Unparenting the Unglued: Reframing Personnel Crises

It's a rare day when a principal glances up from his work to see a teacher weeping in his doorway and muses, "What luck! I was just hoping for a personnel crisis!" But handling personnel crises is a fairly routine part of the job. Eventually some of your most conscientious and talented staffers will end up in your office—unannounced and unglued. They're usually approaching meltdown at worp speed, so it's no use thinking, "*Now*?" or listening with ill-concealed impatience and wondering, "*That's it?*"

Instead, remind yourself that most of these people are simply experiencing a temporary lapse in their coping skills. They've arrived hoping you can fix their problem, absolve them, sympathize, or somehow make them feel better. A brisk round of compassionate coaching will usually get them back on their feet.

> "A leader's role is to raise people's aspirations for what they can become and to release their energies so they will try to get there."
>
> —David Gergen

As an effective professional mentor, your goal is to stabilize them and help them regain control with dignity. So try this. Think of your whole staff as your class. That transforms people-in-crisis into learners. Using the staff-as-students model helps you stay focused on problem solving, and avoid playing Father-knows-best.

Enabling: Eight Steps to Effective Problem Solving

You may have only ten minutes to intervene with a teacher in crisis before the bell rings and the beat goes on. So you'll need to be analytic and efficient. But most of all, you'll need to be an enabler. Now, I know that's a dirty word in psychological circles, where it means "*helping people cling to or perfect their problems.*" You can enable people to get back to work with increased effectiveness. Restoring their ability to perform well with students must be your prime objective. Here are eight steps to positive enabling:

1. *Practice active listening.* This goes way beyond the human tape recorder with a sympathetic face. It's fact-finding. Hang on to every word! As you listen, you'll identify what triggered the crisis and gather clues for effective interventions.

2. *Identify triggers.* The six most common triggers that send functional educators or support staff into a tailspin are: personal workspace changes, student load, limited materials and resources, lack of time, friction with parents or colleagues, and family or health crises. The faster you can identify what triggered the crisis, the sooner you can move on to solutions.

3. *Focus on the doable.* You may hear a grocery list of problems. Be picky. Talk about the ones that are workplace related and will yield to a plan. If you can help people achieve even a 20 percent solution, they usually experience great relief.

4. *Identify strengths.* Remind the employee about other occasions when they have been patient, brilliant, courageous, professional, or reliable. This is critical for their recovery. Listing their strengths—including the courage to seek help—gives them a mental starting point for mastering the situation that sacked them.

5. *Give authentic praise.* Most employees in crisis feel very conflicted. They come to you because they can't cope, but they worry about losing credibility. Restoring self-esteem keeps your relationship intact, so that you can work together on a solution.

6. *Set boundaries.* Think realistically about your part in the solution. Zero in on the most effective thing you can do, but be sure you can deliver. Remember that you're just one part of the solution. Enlist help from the district or your own staff for additional interventions.

7. *Refer to outside resources.* If the issues are serious and personal, suggest that staff consult their therapists, ministers, twelve-step programs such as AA, or the medical profession. Then document your suggestion in a letter to the employee and keep a copy in your file. You may need it later in a grievance, a challenge to an unsatisfactory evaluation, or a wrongful dismissal lawsuit.

8. *Monitor progress.* If the same problem crops up over and over, rethink your interventions and consult a mentor or peer for suggestions. Don't get caught in a ritual of circular conversations, thinking "this time it will be different."

These steps can help you work through most temporary crises with healthy staff members. As a result, they will build trust in you as an effective instructional leader rather than a surrogate parent.

Other Office Visits: Strategies for Chronic Cases

You can count on a cluster of people on any staff that have chronic destabilizing issues recycling through their lives. No matter how hard you work at building a collegial relationship, they want you to play parent as a safety net for their dysfunction. They may initially defer to you, but also struggle with feelings of inferiority, dependence, or passive-aggression that play out like an adolescent testing parental limits. The good news is that very dysfunctional people usually have a limited agenda, so it will only take a few visits for you to get the picture. Here's a list of the usual suspects, and strategies you can use to get them out of your office and back in the game.

Overachievers

Overachievers are good-problem people—usually on your A-list of teachers or support staff. They're idealistic, impatient, achievement-oriented employees who relish a challenge and attack their work with enthusiasm. They are also your high-octane burnouts, because they ask far too much of themselves and wait too long to get help. Overachievers often apologize profusely for falling apart, but respond almost immediately to praise and recognition. Help them rethink their load by assuring them that they're exceeding everyone's expectations except their own, but don't expect them to cut back. It's not in their nature. Regular doses of praise help them maintain a positive outlook.

Sacrificers

Sacrificers clock in early, stay late, and offer themselves to any project that has more work than volunteers. But when they start to hit overload, you pay through the ears. They complain, sometimes loud and long, about their burden and the people who don't do their fair share. Don't tell them to do less and go home early. That's not the point. Sacrificers need to know that you've noticed them, because they crave approval. The most powerful approach to sacrificers is to heap them with legitimate recognition in front of their peers.

Self-Anointed Failures

Self-Anointed Failures collapse in your office, depressed or agitated, and proceed to dismantle themselves. They criticize their performance mercilessly, and then look to you to say it isn't so. I had a teacher open with, "I'm a double failure. I passed the bar, but I never had the courage to practice law. So I got a credential, and now I'm failing at third grade." In fact, this teacher was so excellent with underachievers that parents fought to get their kids in his class. As a result, he was struggling to accommodate twelve different types of learners and feeling overwhelmed. Staffers like this need praise that builds self-esteem, and additional training in the areas where they feel challenged, if only to confirm how much they already know.

Foot Draggers

Foot Draggers are allergic to many of the changes that come with school reform because they're afraid they don't have the skills to succeed in a new system. So they've developed a broad range of responses—none of which actually involve change. Some nod their heads at all the right times, but have no intention of changing. Others work actively behind the scenes to undermine your plans. The more forthright Draggers pout or tantrum. Occasionally, there's a complete meltdown. Self-doubt makes them cling to the old ways like a life preserver. These people need to be coaxed or wooed into testing the waters safely, so success feels better than resistance.

Handle-with-Care Staffers

Handle-with-Care staffers are so emotionally sensitive that they can be crushed by a casual comment or constructive suggestion. Even an impromptu compliment can be misconstrued. If you tell them their hands-on science experiment was very effective, they may conclude that you don't approve of their lecture lessons. If you invite them to observe another teacher doing writer's workshop, they immediately assume their program is flawed. To get inside their safety zone, you need to agree in advance on a structure for your conversations, especially if you will be giving specific feedback or suggestions. They may ask for lots of clarification. With support, they can build confidence in you and hear your compliments and suggestions better.

Dodgers

The Dodger's mantra is *Not my job*. No matter how insignificant the request, if it falls outside their job description, forget about it. You can petition the World Court at the Hague, but they're implacable. Some Dodgers adopt an aggressive work-to-rule stance to demonstrate their resentment toward you or the district. Some use the contract to exert power—albeit a very impotent brand. Others are just lazy or have forgotten why they went into education. Get them trained in a field that interests them, and then have them train the staff.

Filabusters

Filabusters crave attention. They connect with you through conversations, even the one-sided kind where you can't get a word in edgewise. They may start with a remark about the new math curriculum then cover the waterfront, from difficult parents to marital problems. Meanwhile, you're a captive in your own office, struggling to stay afloat on a torrent of syllables. Here's a solution that may seem counterintuitive—like leaning into a punch when you see it coming. But it works. Make regular brief visits to the filabusters' rooms and comment on every good thing you see, keeping the focus tightly on instruction and student progress. Their need for connection and recognition is addressed, and you're free to leave when you want.

Faultfinders

Faultfinders disagree for sport. No matter what is said, they hunt for exceptions, reasons why it won't work, have-you-thought-ofs. Unchallenged, they can suck the life out of any project. Like foot draggers, they may doubt their abilities in a changing workplace, so they protect their personal safety zone through objections. Turn the tables on these energy vampires. Call them into your office and convince them that they're perfect to head up an important project, such as school safety. Provide training to bolster their leadership skills. Once they're in the driver's seat, they'll learn to appreciate people with a positive, can-do attitude.

Rethinking Entitlement

For me, the most compelling reason to avoid a parent-child relationship with staff members is the issue of entitlement. Children feel entitled. They expect to be cared for and loved unconditionally. Everything a parent does—the effort, worry, and sacrifice—is taken for granted, with no thought of reciprocal responsibilities. Entitlement is developmentally appropriate in early childhood, but wreaks havoc in the workplace. It's very difficult to achieve professional expectations, exercise appropriate authority, and, most important, distribute leadership if your staff is locked in an entitlement state of mind. In words and actions, you must convey that your goal is not to nurture a family but to build a team of robust colleagues, determined to provide high-quality learning experiences to all students—because kids are entitled to nothing less.

4
Who's Renting Space in Your Skull?
Getting Smarter About the Minefield Within

- How to Spot a Sapper
- How to Evict a Sapper
- The Seven Deadly Sappers
- How to Stay Positive

Once upon a time there was a principal who sent eighty-one emails to her staff in a single week. They ranged from one-liners to manifestos, some issued only minutes apart. To an outsider, it looked like management by free association. To insiders, it felt like a reign of techno-terror. Harried staffers, dismayed by the high degree of electronic "at you," pounced on the auto-delete and prayed for a virus.

This hyperactive administrator was trying to have a perfect school by peppering her staff with directives. Whenever possible, they fired back. But the skirmishes with her staff were minor compared to the battle she was waging with herself, led by the twin sappers—perfection and control. Sadly, this competent, well-meaning principal was her own worst enemy.

The Enemy Within

Ask most administrators to identify the toughest part of the job and they'll jab the air in the direction of the district office, the faculty lounge, or the Booster Club. I'll bet you can rattle off a list of people who make your work miserable. The whiners, blamers, avoiders, and passive resisters; the undermotivated loafers, and the zealots who announce that the educational sky is falling whenever they have your ear.

Do you fantasize that with just a few involuntary transfers—parents and staff—your school would be heaven? It's not that simple. The people who drive you crazy may, indeed, be teaching in a state of suspended animation, or

29

even bent on your destruction. But other administrators could dismiss them as mildly irritating and go about their business, whereas your reactions run the gamut from moderately ticked off to fully immobilized.

> *"We do not see things as they are. We see things as we are."*
> —The Talmud

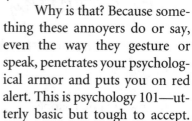

Why is that? Because something these annoyers do or say, even the way they gesture or speak, penetrates your psychological armor and puts you on red alert. This is psychology 101—utterly basic but tough to accept. It's not their *actions*, but *your reactions* that destabilize you. It's possible to work in a war zone, and greet each day with relish—if you're in control of your responses. But if you're ravaged by an army of internal sappers, you can work in a sweetly benign little school and blow yourself to bits from within.

Sappers

Sappers are not the people on your staff who drive you crazy. Sappers are the people—or voices—inside your head that drive you crazy. Sappers are the unconscious beliefs you reinforce with a negative monologue that runs through your head all day long. The voice of the sapper nags, criticizes, terrorizes, at a pitch so etheric that only dogs and your psyche can hear. It says things like: *If you don't get this finished, you'll probably be cleaning out your desk. I can't believe you said that. You looked like an idiot.* Some sappers say *you*, as if they really are a separate entity. Some of us have first-person sappers, who say things like: *I'll do it tomorrow because I work better under pressure. I know they hate me. Nobody cares about this. Why should I?* This negative "self-talk" saps your ability to lead effectively by triggering unhealthy reactions to the people and events around you. Entrenched and unchallenged, sappers destroy your meager peace of mind. At worst, they can detonate your career.

> *"A wise man gets more use from his enemies than a fool from his friends."*
> —Baltasar Gracián

By the time these sappers start making trouble on the job, they've been renting space in your skull for so long that you don't even notice them. They're playing principal-for-a-day, every day, and not doing a particularly good job of it. They run you ragged, and turn your school into your own private minefield. You can surrender to the sappers, or evict them and get on with gardening. It's up to you.

How to Spot A Sapper

Try this experiment. Get a pencil and paper. Say, "people with whom I work," then jot down the first names that come to mind—staffers or community members. Stop after one minute, and take a look. If you're staring at your Ten Most Wanted list, you need to do some housecleaning—in your head.

It's important to understand that these people aren't the sappers. They're informers—pointing you in the direction of your vulnerabilities. So focus on each name on your list. Pay attention to your body's reaction and jot down what you feel. Use these prompts to sharpen your responses.

She reminds me of _____.

He makes me feel _____.

I'm afraid she'll _____.

I wish I could _____.

If it weren't for him _____.

I'd like to tell her _____.

What is the dominant emotion that you experienced? Fear, anger, frustration, avoidance, impotence? Identify that, and you're one step closer to identifying your sappers.

How to Evict a Sapper

To oust a sapper, you have to adopt a brand of hypervigilance that's usually reserved for counterespionage operations and first dates. In other words, you have to notice every little tick and whisper inside your head. You'll be amazed at what you discover. Specifically, you need to

- Train yourself to monitor the negative messages in your head. You'll soon discover that your sapper is running an all-day talk-radio station targeting you. Turn that unconscious voice to full volume, and take notes.

- Challenge the negative messages by cross-examining yourself. Ask questions to debunk the power of your sapper.

- Issue an eviction notice. Decide that your leadership depends on living in a sapper-free zone. Consciously delete every negative statement etched in your head.

- Replace the negative messages with positive statements. Repeat them frequently until they become the dominant voice in your head.

The Seven Deadly Sappers

The Pleaser

Pleasers are driven by a need for approval—being liked is the overriding goal in every interaction. Pleasers avoid confrontation and fear anger, even their

> *"An appeaser is one who feeds a crocodile hoping it will eat him last."*
>
> —Winston Churchill

own. They are well mannered in the face of abuse and excessively grateful. The Pleaser feels guilty just thinking about saying no. You can see why harboring this sapper makes it tough to be a principal. Instead of using your authority appropriately, you're inclined to negotiate, mediate, placate, bargain, compromise, apologize, and reassure. But rather than feeling proud of your diplomatic skills, you're vaguely disappointed each time you duck a tough situation. The Pleaser sends you to the back of your own bus when you should be driving.

The Negative Internal Message. You must be liked by everyone, significant people and bystanders alike. If not, you're a reject.

Questions to Help You Evict the Pleaser

- Do I say yes too often and then feel resentful or overwhelmed?
- What do I think will happen if I say no?
- Is that realistic? Is it disastrous?
- I want to be liked, but can I live without it?
- How will my job be different if some people don't like me?
- If I don't like everyone, why should everyone like me?
- Can I still do my job if some people don't like me?
- If I need to be liked by everyone, I can't be a principal. Which is it going to be?

Positive Replacement Messages

Pleasing myself comes first.

I don't need to be liked to do my job well.

If they don't ask you to drink the hemlock, you're not doing the job.

Persecution is the sincerest form of flattery.

The Critic

The critical sapper is a damning internal voice that constantly finds fault with the things you do. Nothing you do escapes judicial review. You admonish yourself for tiny infractions—a slip of the tongue at a public meeting or a typo in a newsletter, all the while thinking that criticism is a tool of improvement—the harsher the better. The critical sapper plays big-league "If only." *If only I worked harder. If only I got up earlier. If only I had more self-discipline. If only I were smarter.* This constant negative self-appraisal erodes self-esteem and may leave you feeling hopeless. The critic convinces you that you'll never be truly competent.

> *"No one can make you feel inferior without your consent."*
> —Eleanor Roosevelt

The Negative Internal Message. You're not good enough. Try harder.

Questions to Help You Evict the Critical Sapper

- Do I replay small mistakes for days or months?
- Do I feel reluctant to ask questions for fear I'll look uninformed?
- Do I assume everyone knows more than I do?
- Do I exaggerate the competence or credibility of my peers and bosses?
- Do I feel mistakes undermine my professional status?
- Do I feel uncomfortable with praise and shun recognition?
- When things go well, do I say I was just lucky?

Positive Replacement Messages

I do these things very well: _____, _____. (List as many strengths as you can and repeat them out loud several times a day.)

When I focus and use my skills, I am as good as or better than most people.

I can master anything I want.

The Procrastinator

Most procrastinators aren't lazy, or flakes, or disorganized. In fact, some procrastinators are actually misunderstood perfectionists. They don't get things done because they lack the time, information, materials, energy, or logistics to do a task perfectly. So they conclude: *I can't do it perfectly right now, so I'll wait until I can.* Other procrastinators are simply allergic to discomfort, so they work hard at dodging unpleasant duties or emotions. If you hate displays of anger, you probably avoid activities that upset people—such as changing staff assignments or writing up incompetent employees. And since you have a To Do list as long as your arm, it's easy to make a quick detour when an irksome task appears. You just say you're *prioritizing*. Procrastination makes you feel inept or cowardly, and you always have miles to go before you sleep.

The Negative Internal Message. Avoid discomfort as long as possible. Maybe you'll feel more resolute tomorrow, or a better solution will come along to rescue you.

Questions to Help You Evict the Procrastinating Sapper

- What emotions do I have about the thing I'm putting off?
- Am I avoiding it because I resent having to do it?
- Is this my way of saying no?
- Whose task is this, anyway?
- Am I avoiding it because I don't know how to handle it?
- Do I think I have to do it perfectly? How little will be enough?
- Do I have everything I need to tackle this?
- Who could help me with the missing parts?
- What part of this can I do now?
- How would I feel if I had already started this?

Positive Replacement Messages

A good plan today is better than a perfect plan tomorrow.
It won't kill me to do it for five minutes.
If I tackle projects in pieces, I can do some parts with ease.
All progress is progress.

The Perfectionist

Perfectionists come off as critical, rigid, easily upset with their own mistakes, unappreciative, unrealistic, and obsessive compulsive. In short, not a good person to work for. Worse, not a good person to be. Perfectionists expect the impossible from themselves, then eat themselves alive worrying that they can't achieve their expectations. So if you are a perfectionist, you rarely give yourself credit for all the things you've done well, and everyone around you ends up feeling unappreciated because nothing is ever good enough to satisfy you.

Perfectionists are driven by a sense of inadequacy that makes them hypersensitive to criticism. They can't use it constructively because it reinforces their sense of personal failure. Perfectionism convinces you that you're never good enough, but makes it almost impossible for you to admit mistakes and get help.

The Negative Internal Message. You must consistently demonstrate competence at a very high level. Otherwise, you're a failure as a person.

Questions to Help You Evict the Perfectionist Sapper

- Is there really a perfect way to do this task?
- Does it need to be perfect to be effective?
- If it's not perfect, what will happen?
- Would it be realistic to expect this level of performance from anyone else?
- What scares me about being un-perfect?
- Am I basing my self-worth on being perfect?
- Do I equate being perfect with being professionally credible?
- What's the worst thing that can happen if I'm un-perfect from time to time?
- Would I want a boss like me?

Positive Replacement Messages

I do many things very well.

I usually do far more than my colleagues expect.

If I want, I can learn skills that will help me perform better, but I'm already excellent in many ways.

The Cynic

Cynics live in a perpetual cringe. They are puzzled by optimism and convince themselves that their wary attitude is just good emergency perparedness.

"I told you so" is a favorite phrase. While waiting for the other shoe to drop, they confidently forecast all the negative possibilities. Principals who are given to cynicism are afraid to be publicly enthusiastic or passionate. You'll rarely find them out on an educational limb for fear that the great lumbering bureaucracy will cut off their support and they'll be in a free fall without a net.

Cynicism is also a haven for principals who have run out of steam. They camouflage their lethargy with anecdotes to demonstrate that nothing ever changes—why try? Cynicism keeps you from taking action to improve things and alienates you from energetic, innovative peers.

The Negative Internal Message. The system is flawed. If it were going to get better, it would have done so long ago. Look at all the people who are smarter and work harder than me. What does it get them?

Questions to Help You Evict the Cynical Sapper

- Now that I've imagined the worst, what would it be like to imagine the best?
- What would I do if I was sure I would succeed?
- What's the downside of being an optimist?
- What does being cynical get me?
- Do I use cynicism as a cover for a lack of courage?
- Do I act cynical because I'm afraid I don't have the skills to effect change if I tried?

Positive Replacement Messages

You should always go farther than you should go.

Nothing succeeds like excess.

The Worrier

Worriers play all-star "But what if . . . ?" Their favorite decision-making tool is the crystal ball. They peer in and see catastrophes—never good news. They distort their world by maximizing potential problems and minimizing their ability to solve them. When not looking into the future, worriers look over employees' shoulders, spreading anxiety and eroding trust. So if you're a worrier, you need to give up the séance approach and get real. Worrying prevents you from feeling safe in the present, no matter how good life is. The worried sapper thrives on uncertainty or potential danger, and convinces you that obsessing on these possibilities is armor against disaster.

The Negative Internal Message. The possibilities for disaster are always there. If I don't worry about it, the worst will probably happen.

Questions to Help You Evict the Worried Sapper

- What am I telling myself?
- What are the facts?
- How likely are my worries?
- Do I think of worry as a way of baby-sitting unfinished business until I can get to it: "I'm not ignoring this. I worry about it all the time"?
- Is worrying a way to keep myself revved up but without any productive outcome?
- Does worrying do any good? Is it a form of working through that leads to insights, or does it just tie up my attention and my stomach?

Positive Replacement Messages

It's too early to worry about this since it may never happen.

Maybe later I'll have some more solutions.

Doing feels better than worrying.

What's one thing I can do to improve the outcome?

The Controller

Controllers need to be in charge of the people and events around them. They may look confident and bossy, but in reality they're driven by a fear of failure, so they hoard decisions and act in haste before other people have a chance to make decisions—and mistakes. Controllers don't care much for introspection, but they are blessed with an immense capacity for continuous pressure and follow-through on projects.

If you're harboring a controlling sapper, you may like to work alone, without consulting support staff or teachers. You may have a hard time delegating, and resent the popularity of consensus building. It takes a lot of time, and there's no guarantee you'll get the outcome you want. Your private notion of shared decision making is "I've made a decision, now I'll share it." But a word of caution: overcontrolled employees are ripe for passive agression or open revolt. Insisting on control is a recipe for frustration and disappointment on all sides.

The Negative Internal Message. Problems are caused by other people's mistakes. Controlling them is self-protection. I'm the only one who can do it right.

Questions to Help You Evict the Controlling Sapper

- Are my expectations realistic?
- Do I demand compliance when it isn't necessary?
- Is this a battle of wills?
- Is being in control a tool for being perfect?
- Do I trust other people to do the right thing?
- Do I hoard control so I can hoard the credit?
- What scares me about losing control?
- What is the value of sharing control?
- What do I lose by controlling staff?
- Would I want a boss like me?

Positive Replacement Statements

I've been smart enough to surround myself with competent people. I can trust them with some decisions.

I can share decisions without losing control.

How to Stay Positive

All sappers have a negative impact on your ability to lead. None of them are cheerleaders; none accurately assess your strengths or goodness. To combat these private demons, develop the habit of willfully and persistently prospecting for what's right in your world. Strengthen your mind to resist the gravity of negative people and situations around you. Invent the world you want to live in by starting your day with an optimistic litany and shifting your focus back to the positive after every negative encounter, no matter how small. On your way to work, ask yourself

- What's good about today?
- Who's happy that I'm the administrator of this school?
- Who is doing better because I'm the principal?
- Where can I have the most impact today?
- How can I have some fun?

After a negative encounter, ask yourself

- What can I learn from this?
- What have I done well today?

- What's the best thing I did all week?
- Who is excellent on the staff? How can I let that person know?
- Who needs me on the staff? How can I give that person a boost?
- Where can I see my vision in living color?

The Big Reason to Evict Your Sappers

There are successful people in every walk of life who say, "I owe it all to my neurosis!" You may be one of them, convinced that your sapper is not a problem, but your secret weapon. After all, what kind of a principal would you be if you didn't relentlessly worry, control, or placate?

Well, you'd be more effective. More likely to succeed. Less prone to burning out or being fired. That's right. The literature on leadership indicates that the most effective leaders possess what psychologists refer to as an internal locus of control. If you have an internal locus of control, you approach your work with a sense of personal strength, confident that you can achieve your goals. You know how to direct your ability, focus your effort, and summon the motivation needed to tackle and complete tough tasks. In other words, you can count on yourself to handle the challenges of your job. If you fail, that's also your doing. You are reflective, honest, and not afraid to ask for help.

By contrast, if you have an *external* locus of control, you think that your success or failure depends on people or circumstances largely beyond your control—the difficulty of the work, the lack of skill or will in others, bad luck, or unfavorable political conditions. You never know from one moment to the next what will go wrong, how wrong it will go, and how damaged you will be by the repercussions. If your idea of a solution is to change the other guy, you're not leading—you're arm wrestling. And you will continue to do so until one of you retires, relocates, or wanders into the path of the Number 9 bus. You can't change the people around you, but you can learn from them, and change yourself. You can reach your potential as leader, but only if you take charge of the space inside your skull.

5

Hire the Best

Getting Smarter About Selecting Staff

- Paper Screening
- Cold Calling
- Team Hiring
- Preparing for Interviews
- Writing Effective Questions
- Keeping Your Questions Legal
- Writing Prompts

- Interviewing Techniques
- Demonstration Lessons
- Reference Checks
- Notifying Unsuccessful Candidates
- Hiring Nonteaching Staff
- Hiring a Coadministrator

The day my district adopted class-size reduction, I was lounging on a beach in North Carolina, fitful, twitching, unaccustomed to the silence. Having survived the first year of my principalship, I was ready for a long spell of sloth. A week later I was back in my office, knee-deep in resumes and dialing for teachers. No beach time, no novels. Just an outrageous opportunity for gardening. In a mere six weeks, I would add eleven amazing people to my staff. It was the best unvacation a principal ever had.

For administrators in many districts, hiring has become a spectator sport as unions increasingly negotiate to control staffing. The New York City Teachers' Contract presents an arresting example of this upside-down world, where principals can't hire but must supervise and evaluate. When a vacancy occurs, tenured teachers from any school may apply, and the one with the most seniority gets the job. End of discussion. The principal is so marginalized that the transferring teacher is not even required to show up before the first day of school.

So, if you need to read this chapter, consider yourself lucky. If you get to fill three vacancies two weeks before school starts, stand up and cheer, because you're still in possession of the right to hire—the most powerful tool in the gardener's shed!

Your Partners in Human Resources

The human resources department in your district is there to help—in fact, you can't get the job done without them. But they don't take hiring personally. They work in an office, on the receiving end of hundreds of phone calls a day, plus an avalanche of resumes and applications. Think pegs in holes and you get the goal of personnel. Whether you end up with the world's best teacher, or a nutcase with an expired emergency credential, their job is largely unchanged. Even if you get no teacher at all, they'll still be working in a relatively serene office, whereas, you could be facing twenty first graders, all shined up for the first day of school, and a substitute teacher whose usual beat is high school calculus. Or escorting a professional musician-turned-substitute-teacher to an AP chemistry lab. It's your problem, and it's very personal. So roll up your sleeves, and hire, hire, hire. It's a contact sport!

> *"I have come to believe that a great teacher is a great artist, and that there are as few as there are any other great artists. Teaching might even be the greatest of arts since the medium is the human mind and spirit."*
>
> —John Steinbeck

Paper Screening

The first step in hiring excellent staff is gleaning vital information hidden in a stack of resumes. You can whittle a field of potential candidates down to your Ten Most Desirable List in an hour or so if you study every application as if it were the Rosetta stone, and always read between the lines.

- The best indicator of what a person will do for you is what he has done elsewhere. If you see a half page of committee work and community service, you've got an activist on your hands. If you're looking for a spark plug, put this one in the interview pile.

- Focus on verifiable facts: positions held, responsibilities, dates, and salaries. Do the math. If there are significant gaps in the dates of employment or no dates at all, pay attention. If the last salary is significantly higher or lower than the job for which the person is applying, check it out. The phone is your friend in the prehiring process. If you have a hunch that something is amiss, contact some of the references or a former employer. A few minutes of detective work can help you thin the pile or zero in on a winner.

- Search for evidence of knowledge, skills, and ability in every possible place in the application, including reference letters, undergraduate minors, and special interests.

- Weigh the strengths but search for weaknesses—a narrow band of experience, no evidence of growth, no team work, or a half dozen experiences all in short succession. Marginal applicants mask deficiencies with ambiguities or omissions. I've yet to see "I was fired" gracing an application.

- Letters of recommendation are packed with clues about candidates. I read them with a yellow highlighter in hand, so I can mark key phrases for reference during an interview. First, check the dates. Three-year-old letters are not a good sign. Next, look for a letter from the most recent supervisor. If it's missing, ask for it. Recommendations from a broad spectrum of colleagues indicate a robust professional life beyond the classroom. Finally, I look for passion and originality in letters of recommendation. Safe language may mean that the writer wouldn't walk the plank for this person.

Don't paper-screen alone. Recruit colleagues who know the requirements of the job to lend their eyes to the effort. They can spot things that you miss, and act as a sounding board while you think through the complex dynamics of adding a new person to the staff.

Cold Calling

Now you have a stack of "good paper." Don't even think about hiring at this point—it could only lead to grief. When I finish paper screening, I sit down with the pile of "possibles," pour a cup of coffee, and start dialing. Before you say "forget it," you should know that the thought of calling a stranger used to horrify me. But during that summer hiring marathon, I learned to love it. Cold calls saved me hours of pointless interviews and kept good people from being scooped up by other districts. I've actually intercepted people on the brink of signing a contract and convinced them to see me first.

Cold calls provide a flesh-and-blood sense of the candidates, but they have to be efficient. I don't want to spend the whole afternoon on the phone with one applicant, so I ask two or three questions that get to the heart of the matter, like:

- Tell me about your most recent teaching experience.
- How do you identify and respond to individual learning differences?
- What are the most important things you can do to help students succeed?

- How would your students or colleagues describe you? Your supervisor?
- Tell me about the strategies you use to help students succeed in
  _____.
- What experience have you had with inclusion of special education students?
- What assessment techniques have you used?
- Describe ways that you incorporate projects and hands-on activities in your curriculum.

Then I listen for key words, thinking versus jargon, and most of all, energy. I want an exciting professional dialogue. If I hear passion, eagerness, even irreverence, I'm all ears. And fingers. I scribble notes all over the application to capture my impressions. This process may go on for days before I get a good crop of candidates.

Cold calls give me first crack at shaping the candidate list. I can reject people for lots of reasons without a discussion. Only the winners in my dialing-for-dollars festival are invited to interview.

Team Hiring

As a principal, I never hired alone. I hired teachers with teachers, clerks with my administrative assistants, custodians with my plant manager, assistant principals with staff and other administrators. I've also been on hiring teams that included parents, mentors, community representatives, and university colleagues.

When recruiting season rolled around, I extended invitations to the entire staff to join the hiring team, then crossed my fingers. I cringed at the thought of who might accept my offer, but I was determined to avoid the accusation that I was rigging the process. I also trolled for volunteers and got lucky every time. I hired with a team because I valued their expertise and dedication. I wanted to build an outstanding staff, they wanted the best colleagues. We all refused to settle for second best, even when summer was long in the tooth. It was a very bonding experience. After one spectacular interview,

> *"One measure of leadership is the caliber of people who choose to follow you."*
>
> —Dennis Peer

my team shouted, "don't let her out of the building without a contract." Their cries were music to my ears, because it meant they owned that hire. As a result, every newcomer on the staff had his or her own cheering section, starting from day one.

Another advantage of team hiring is that great teams attract great candidates. Smart candidates know that their colleagues can make or break them, so it's easier for them to evaluate your offer and say yes if they spend time with a half dozen of your brightest and best teachers, who clearly like you and each other. Team hiring is the most effective way to sell your school to outstanding applicants who may have three or four offers.

Of course, you are the only one who can make the final hiring decisions, because you bear the responsibility for supervision and evaluation of all employees. So take a few minutes to remind your hiring team that there may be times when one person will disagree with the rest of the team. Talk about why that might happen, and how they feel about it. You may need to agree that the dissenting voice on the team will not leave in a huff and bad-mouth a successful candidate in the faculty lounge. Then remind them that even if they are wild about a candidate, you may uncover information during the reference check that could disqualify the person. Again, that would be your judgment call, and they need to trust that you are doing what is best for the school.

Preparing for Interviews

The challenge of interviewing is to get the best out of every candidate in a limited amount of time. Effective interviews are focused, strategic investigations that feel like collegial conversations. The first step in preparing for interviews is to think about what you need. I don't mean a first-grade teacher or a baseball coach. What do you need to build a strong, smart staff? Do you need another teacher-leader, some innovative collaborators, or shock troops?

Next, hone a list of legal questions exploring attitudes and practices that you consider deal makers or breakers. I recommend six to eight open-ended questions for a forty-five minute interview. Good questions allow candidates to think out loud, provide detailed answers, even raise questions of their own. That doesn't happen if you pepper them with yes or no questions at the rate of one per minute.

Writing Effective Questions

If you're working with a team, they usually have their own high-priority questions that focus on philosophy, pedagogy, or instructional experience. You need to probe for ethics, strengths, and dedication—the heart of the candidate. Work together to craft a balanced set of questions, using this list to jump-start the process.

Sample Questions for Teaching Candidates

- To begin, please tell us what we should know about your experience and training that make you an excellent candidate for this job.
- How do you recognize and respond to individual learning differences?
- How do you adjust your lessons so that all students can succeed?
- Tell us about your experience with school improvement work, curriculum development, teaming, multiage teaching, looping?
- What strategies are needed to help special education students succeed?
- What is your understanding of IDEA (Individuals with Disabilities Education Act) and Section 504?
- What are some assessment strategies that you have used?
- Describe an effective assessment technique for limited-English speakers.
- How do you incorporate critical thinking into your teaching?
- Tell us about your approach to discipline.
- If we could walk into your classroom, what would we see?
- What is the most important thing you do as a teacher to help kids succeed?
- What special talents or skills would you bring to the staff?
- How do you communicate with the parents of your students?
- How do you alert parents to problems between reporting periods?
- How do you train and use volunteers?
- How do you engage students in service learning?
- What words would your students use to describe you?
- What is your greatest strength as a teacher?
- What is your area of greatest challenge?
- What is your focus for professional growth?
- What traits do you appreciate in colleagues and team members?
- We've come to the end of our questions. Is there anything else that you would like us to know about your qualifications for this job?
- Do you have any questions for us?

Throw in a few situational questions, such as

- Suppose a parent came to you insisting that the grade you gave their child is too low. How would you address their concern?

- A student is on a 504 plan for ADHD. What types of accommodations might you suggest to help the student focus during your class?
- You're teaching freshman composition but discover that several of your students speak English as a second language and need basic writing skills. What instructional strategies would you use to meet these students at their level and to ensure significant progress?

Tweak these questions to fit your needs, then give them the civil rights test.

Keeping Your Questions Legal

Here's a simple is-it-legal test. Ask yourself: *Is the question related to the essential functions of the job?* Costly lawsuits have been filed against districts because interviewers innocently strayed into personal territory. Questions like: "Do you have any kids?" "When did you graduate from Akron High?" "That's an interesting name—is it Persian?" can be construed by applicants as a screen for discrimination. The job requirements must be the focus of the question. If not, rephrase or drop it. Train your team using these examples:

Legal: Do you have any commitments that would prevent you from staying for faculty meetings until five o'clock twice a month?

Not: Do you have young kids who need to be picked up at a certain time?

Legal: Do you have any health issues that would prevent you from carrying a full teaching load?

Not: Teaching is very stressful. Have you ever had psychological problems?

Legal: Tell us about your graduate studies at Bernadine College.

Not: I see you went to Bernadine College. Is that Catholic?

Legal: What languages do you speak or read fluently?

Not: Is Tagalog your native language?

Writing Prompts

Written communication is a critical skill for teachers. In some communities, parents and teachers keep in touch almost exclusively through notes, newsletters, emails, and narratives. So you may want to include a writing sample in your hiring process. Ask candidates to come in thirty minutes before their interview to complete the writing sample and emphasize that it's only a draft. Provide a computer and printer, since many of us are losing the knack of composing by hand—and the samples will be easier for your team to read.

Sample Writing Prompts for Teaching Candidates

- Literacy is the goal of our school. Write a letter to parents giving them tips on helping their children strengthen literacy skills at home.
- You're starting a difficult unit of instruction. Write a letter to parents explaining what students will learn and how they will be assessed.
- You are having behavioral problems with a student. List the steps you would take to find a solution.
- Your students will be taking standardized tests/exit exams/finals next month. Write a letter to parents explaining the purpose of the tests, how they interface with your curriculum, and the best ways for students to prepare.
- Your department has revised its curriculum to reflect state standards. Write a letter to parents explaining the relationship between state standards and student success.

Interviewing Techniques

Once you've polished your questions and writing prompts, have a member of your support staff confirm all appointments, so that you won't waste time waiting for no-shows. At the start of each interview, have the team introduce themselves, then let the candidate in on the game. Share your format—who will be asking the questions, who will be scribe, the number of questions you want to ask, and how much time is allotted for the whole process. Have a clock visible so candidates can budget their time. Tell applicants that there will be time at the end of the interview for them to share additional information and ask their own questions.

Interviews are highly subjective affairs, easily influenced by appearance, mannerisms, and verbal skills. Work against this inherent unfairness by asking all the applicants the same questions. If a clever person gives a superficial answer about assessment, and a quiet candidate is encyclopedic in her response, the team will be able to get beyond the glitter or lackluster and look at the evidence of knowledge. The team can make better decisions when they focus on the content and quality of the responses—in effect, comparing apples to apples.

I know it's been a good interview when the team members

- add to their professional knowledge through the process;
- treat the candidate as a resource by asking to know more;
- are eager to spend more time with the candidate;
- feel their time was well spent.

Demonstration Lessons

My teams quickly learned that a good interview is just that—an interview. Talking is important, but expert instruction is a must. After an impressive interview, we still insisted on seeing the real thing, even if we had to raid the day-care center or teen club for an audience. Don't skip demonstration lessons. You owe it to the students who could spend 180 days—1,400 precious hours—with this candidate.

The simplest solution is to make a site visit. Go to the candidates' classes and see them in action. If that's not possible, round up a group of kids in the approximate age range of the position you're trying to fill. In the very heart of summer, I'd get the PTA president on the phone and beg her to find a dozen kids. The deal was that we would feed and entertain the kids for two hours, leaving the moms or baby-sitters unexpectedly free. Or you can arrange with a summer school principal to have a "guest teacher"—your candidate—take over for a period. We drove to other districts. We would have crossed state lines to get the right person.

Demonstration lessons aren't long—thirty to forty-five minutes is enough. Look for the ability to establish rapport, exert appropriate control, engage kids in a thinking process, and motivate them to learn. Most of the time demonstrations confirm your hunches. Occasionally, we saw a really bad lesson and were grateful for the chance to keep searching.

Reference Checks

If you think you have a keeper, make haste carefully. Great candidates often interview with three or four districts at once, and become disenchanted by a series of delays. But you must check references. So be encouraging to strong candidates, and then get on the phone. If the personnel department offers to make the calls for you, say no. First of all, it may take days for them to get to your candidates. In the meantime, your dream teacher may say yes to a district that moves faster or seems more organized. More important, there's a lot to be learned in a five-minute call if you ask the right questions. Don't leave this to chance. Ask your personnel office for a reference-check form or use these questions to help you make your final decision.

Key Questions for Reference Checks

- When you call, introduce yourself, explain the purpose of the call, and ask if the person has five or ten minutes to spend with you.
- Confirm the relationship of the applicant to the reference. Some people actually list friends as references, knowing that some districts are just too busy to call.
- Ask about the responsibilities and performance of the candidate.
- Ask about strengths and weaknesses.
- Ask how a new supervisor could help this person improve.
- Ask for three words that would best characterize this person.
- Ask if there were attendance problems.
- Be direct. Ask if the person would rehire the candidate, given the opportunity.
- Thank the person for taking the time to speak with you.

If you still have some doubts, don't stop at the reference list. Call other people who may have vital information to share, such as a faculty member at the applicant's university. Take notes during each call and hang on to them. If your decision to hire or decline is ever challenged, you'll need them. Listen for pauses, vagueness, spin-doctoring, sidestepping. The speaker may be dying to unload this person. If you feel the answers are evasive, be blunt. The candidate and your students are hanging in the balance. This is your last chance to avoid a mistake.

Never skip reference checks. I've known principals who did, only to learn that their new addition to the staff had been fired in two other districts. The cost of hiring a dud skyrockets when you calculate the hours you'll devote to fruitless coaching, evaluating, and placating unhappy parents. Then you have to fill the position all over again after a grueling dismissal. A few phone calls can save a lot of grief.

Notifying Unsuccessful Candidates

Calling the winners is a treat because it's the start of something wonderful. But informing the runners-up is difficult, especially if you've spent hours interviewing and observing a promising candidate. You may be inclined to avoid this step, so get a system in place that works for you. The most efficient approach is to write a form letter and have your administrative assistant send it out immediately after you make your decision. Your letter will probably cross paths in the mail with a thank-you note from the hopeful candidate, since most are well trained in employment protocol. The letter should be generic—thank the candidate for applying, indicate that you have chosen a different person, and wish the person the best of luck in the profession. Include an invitation to call for more feedback on their interview. Your notes provide specific details on strengths and areas for growth that could help the candidate succeed the next time around.

Phone calls are faster and more personal, except for the machines that cheerfully answer at least half the time. Occasionally you owe the person—and the profession—a personal call. My team was horrified when a talented candidate told us the she would have had a more successful first year if she'd had a better class—of kids. She went on to describe the racial and ethnic makeup of her students, in terms that bordered on racism. Later that day, I dialed, prayed for a machine, but got her in person. It was a hard conversation. She was shocked, but open enough to hear the perceptions of the team and mature enough to thank me for the feedback.

Hiring Nonteaching Staff

Support staff are often the school's invisible army. They clean, cook, type, file, shelve, sort, supervise, mop brows, apply Band-Aids, mow, blow, and rake—largely unapplauded. It just takes a nurse with attendance problems or a cafeteria manager with a lousy sense of timing to throw an entire school into chaos, so hiring nonteaching staff deserves quality time and attention. If you routinely delegate support-staff interviews to others, it sends a message about hierarchy and status. "She's too busy to interview custodians." Remember, a good plant manager can reduce campus complaints and unhappiness by 50 percent. Although you may never get credit for a brilliant hire, you'll certainly get the blame if the campus is littered and the rooms are unswept. Here a few tips for making a success of it.

- Call in the experts. Hiring support staff may require knowledge outside your comfort zone. Quizzing a maintenance candidate about plumbing emergencies can make you feel like the great imposter. So invite the experts on campus who do that job to join the interview team. They'll be able to spot a good answer from a clunker, and feel valued to be part of the process.

- Call the central office staff who train and supervise support staff. Ask them to sit in on the interviews, or if that's not possible, buy them a cup of coffee and find out what questions they'd ask. Many departments have sample interview questions that they'll gladly share. After all, they want a strong workforce, too.

- Central office managers are eager to share their expertise, and feel flattered when you ask for advice. In the process, you build a better working relationship for the times when you need their help. But most important, you lessen the possibility of hiring a dud. If you do make a mistake, you can undo it together.

Hiring a Coadministrator

Selecting a coadministrator or assistant principal can be one of the most perilous tasks in the principal's job description. The relationship between coadministrators is complex and multifaceted—at times, eerily like a marriage. Coadministrators routinely share twelve-hour days, six days a week, filled with tough tasks and unexpected triumphs. It affects people in life-changing ways.

When coadministrators respect and trust each other, the whole is greater than the sum of the parts. Without it, leadership can disintegrate into arm wrestling or steely silence. A dysfunctional relationship between administrators can undermine the entire foundation of a learning community. How can you anticipate problems and avoid making a bad choice? Be realistic about the potential for problems. In your euphoria at the thought of having someone to ease your burden, you may forget that an assistant principal will need time, coaching, and evaluation. If you are one of the few principals in the country testing the coprincipal hypothesis, the challenge of sharing power equitably is even greater. Some of the barriers to coadministration are different core values, incompatible leadership styles, unclear roles, competition for the top spot, breakdown in communication, and a lack of commitment to mutual goals.

To clarify what you want, and what you can live with in a coadministrator, use the successful relationships in your life as a guide. Develop a list of the attributes you value in a partner or colleague—courage, loyalty, hard work, a sense of humor, responsibility, and putting kids first, even when it hurts.

Now spend some time thinking about how things can go wrong. What bugs you? What's your greatest weakness in a relationship? What's your greatest strength? What do you absolutely need to make sharing the burden an adventure rather than a chore?

Finally, think about your personal leadership style. Are you rule driven, with a love of structure, boundaries, and a clear game plan? Or do you need the big picture and a firm grip on the meaning and implications of the work before you can move forward? Is action your middle name—stop talking and get to the bottom line? Or are feelings at the top of your agenda—sharing, caring, and supporting must be the foundation for any meaningful work?

People who analyze leadership styles tend to identify four basic categories. You may have done a leadership exercise where participants divide themselves into north, south, east, or west categories based on a series of statements. Other sorting systems use idealist, strategist, tactician, and administrator. The labels don't matter. What's important is to identify your leadership bent and find complementary colleagues. Here are four general types. This is a rough guide, meant only to help you analyze your basic leadership instincts before embarking on the search for a partner.

Type 1: I Love People

I-love-people types ore fascinated with people. They are value driven, patient, respectful, personal, inspirational, intuitive. Most are comfortable working outside the system and show a high tolerance for ambiguity. They take criticism personally and avoid confrontation but enjoy the role of mentor and facilitator. Relationships shaped their goals.

Type 2: I Love Plans

Plan people are fascinated with concepts and facts. They are criteria driven, fiercely independent, intellectual, mentally restless, serious, competitive, and loners. They rely on criteria and guidelines, use an objective, analytic approach to situations, and prefer ambiguity to routine tasks. These future-oriented persons shape their goals by long-range priorities and tasks.

Type 3: I Love a Challenge

People who love a challenge are fascinated with action. They are impulsive risk takers, who live in the moment. They are also perfectionists, playful, hands-on, and skillful. Easily bored with schedules and systems, they are excellent in a crisis, great problem solvers, flexible, and opportunity driven. They are gifted negotiators. Individualists, they need freedom to explore outside the box. They focus on immediate challenges as their goals.

Type 4: I Love Systems

Systems people love structure. They are workaholics who are goal driven, punctual, precise, productive, and efficient. Finishing is the most important part of the task. These people are excellent at providing tools for teams to get the job done, but they are traditionalists, who enjoy the security of routines and need order and predictability. Their goals are shaped by desire to refine, improve, and develop known systems in the near future.

Using these thumbnail sketches can help you define your comfort zone and identify must-have characteristics in a potential coadministrator. There is no single formula for success, but acknowledging the fundamental features of your own leadership style may help you strike an interesting balance with your partner, and avoid the oil-and-water approach to school administration. With this self-knowledge in hand, you're better equipped to sort through the candidates.

Looking for Mr./Ms./Mrs. Right

During the hunt for a coadministrator, it's easy to be dazzled by a resume with a long list of accomplishments, especially if they end in "at Harvard University," followed by dates more recent than your last dental exam. If you need a dictionary to plow through the adjectives attributed to the aspirant, cast a jaundiced eye. Sometimes a candidate's apparent virtues are really the tip of an iceberg, and you're the *Titanic*. Here are some red flags. Watch for them.

Workaholics

People who routinely turn in seventy- to eighty-hour weeks may be unorganized, perfectionists, miserable in their personal lives, or totally lacking a personal life. None of those characteristics are about doing the job well, and they surely aren't the stuff of a good partner. You could find yourself on the receiving end of a load of resentment if you call it quits after a measly sixty hours, or draw the line at coming in on Saturday *and* Sunday. You could knock yourself out and still be cast in the role of the sluggard because you can't live up to the expectations of a hyperactive partner.

"Her Door Is Always Open"

A peson who is always accessible may be someone who has great public relations instincts. It could also mean the person loses focus, can't prioritize, has problems with time management, or is too meek to say no. A coadministrator who's there for anyone, anytime, can undermine your efforts to set boundaries with the staff and community.

A Rising Star

Stars are usually risk takers and go-getters, with impressive skills in self-promotion. You need to ask, "Is this person rising by virtue of accomplishments and personal character or, like a zeppelin, via hot air?" Some stars are just good talkers who can't deliver or aren't interested in getting their hands dirty. What they crave is an audience and a promotion. You may be seen as the competition, or a stepping stone on their way to the top. One aspiring administrator told a colleague, "I'm heading for the Hill (central office). If you get in my way, I'll flatten you!" Check references!

"Everyone Loves Him"

If you hear that everyone loves your candidate, it may indicate a person who needs to please more than he needs to lead. You can put money down that he will cozy up to the whiners on the staff, with whom you've taken a hard line, and get plenty of strokes for being sympathetic. He'll do for staff what they should do for themselves, just to win points. People who want to be universally liked don't belong in administration. If you hire one, you may find yourself alone on the firing line, undermined from within, and the only one who doesn't "love" your coadministrator.

Just Leave It to Me

Hyperresponsible people can shoulder huge amounts of responsibility as long as you stay out of the way. Their need for control drives them to charge ahead, starting and finishing projects all by themselves. This puts a strain on partners who prefer a thoughtful, collaborative approach. While getting the job done, they may run roughshod over other people's good ideas, wielding their power with little thought for staff or their coadministrator.

Born Competitors

Some people must be the fastest, smartest, and best at everything, which makes it hard for them to co-anything. Competitive people need to take the credit, even if you did all the work. Or they play up their skills, and forget to mention yours. Comments like, "I'm the techy. She can't even turn on a printer," capture the essence of this relationship. Competitive colleagues sabotage their partners and portray themselves as the only thing keeping the ship afloat.

Finding the Right Fit

Sample Questions for Coadministrators

- What do you think qualifies you to succeed at this job?
- What makes a job satisfying to you?
- How do you feel about being closely or loosely supervised?
- What did you dislike about your most recent job?
- What did you do to change it?
- Tell us about a successful innovation that you initiated to help students.
- What are your strengths as a manager?
- What are your strengths as a leader?
- What are your strengths in curriculum and assessment?
- What is your supervisory style?
- Tell us about a time when you had to deal with a substandard employee. How did you assist and/or discipline the employee? How did the employee respond?
- Tell us about a career accomplishment of which you are most proud.
- What are your goals for the next two years? Five years?

Most districts hire administrators at the central-office level. The process is similar to hiring teachers, but the panels may be larger and the questions more complex, with the superintendent and union president involved in the final decision. Your role will vary from one district to another. You may sit on all the committees or just one. When the field narrows to the final candidates, advocate strongly for site visits. It's critical to see potential partners on their home turf and to interview coworkers. And don't be afraid to ask for additional interviews or informal conversations before a deal is struck. After all, you're the one who will be living with this person fifty to sixty hours per week. Getting this right can make the difference between loving your job and eagerly scanning the classifieds.

Holding Out for the Best

Finally, remember that hiring is a personal investment that affects every member of your school community. It requires research, focus, intuition, and courage. Never resort to drive-by hiring, no matter how desperate your situation seems. The payoff for your persistence is that kids get the best shot at learning, and the foundation of your school gets stronger. Hiring excellent teachers, support staff, or coadministrators is one of the supreme joys of gardening.

6

The Fezziwig Principle

Getting Smarter About Motivating Staff

- Recognition
- Relationships
- Resources
- Rewards
- Rituals

John Shambra was eccentric, as administrators go. His office boasted an upright piano and little else. Each morning his staff left a neatly typed list of song titles on the bench. Each afternoon, he gave an impromptu concert while they completed their paperwork. During a teachers' strike, he herded 120 kids into an auditorium the size of a living room and, five days later, they were a chorus. Returning teachers were greeted by the sweet strains of "Dona Nobis Pacem."

John convinced us to schedule parent conferences at night by hosting a gourmet dinner in our World War II cafeteria. When we arrived, word-weary and starving, we were greeted with tablecloths, flowers, and John, serving the best pasta that kitchen had every seen. He squired immigrant parents around the community to practice their English, transformed dingy hallways with giant mural projects, and never met a rascal he didn't like.

Dozens of passionate teachers, me included, trailed him from urban outpost to inner-city school to enjoy his benevolent leadership. He was Fezziwig. We were his followers. The rest—location, commute, colleagues—were just incidentals

The original Fezziwig, created by Charles Dickens in *A Christmas Carol* (1844), was also an extraordinary boss. We see him through the eyes of Ebenezer Scrooge, who was about as bad a boss as you can imagine—stingy, critical, and mean. His solitary employee, Bob Cratchett, was frightened all the time. By contrast, Fezziwig is adored, especially for his Christmas parties. Eavesdropping on this cheerful event, the Ghost of Christmas Past comments derisively to Scrooge,

A small matter to make these silly folk so full of gratitude. He has spent but a few pounds of your mortal money: three or four perhaps. Is that so much that he deserves this praise?

Scrooge rushes to Fezziwig's defense.

It isn't that, Spirit. He has the power to render us happy or unhappy: to make our service light or burdensome: a pleasure or a toil. Say that his power lies in words and looks, in things so slight and insignificant that it is impossible to add and count 'em up; what then? The happiness he gives is quite as great as if it cost a fortune.

Good managers, like Mr. Fezziwig and Mr. Shambra, use dozens of small acts to cheer and motivate employees. In most cases, the gratitude of staff members far outweighs the time or expense required. This chapter outlines the five Rs of Fezziwigging— strategies you can use to brighten employees' attitudes and boost performance.

Recognition

Schools are the natural habitat of gold stars, A pluses, and the honor roll. Some teachers have raised positive reinforcement to the level of an art form, convinced that they can make a scholar out of a sad sack with an unstinting stream of "good job!" and "great!" And they do, because kids are highly susceptible to praise. Lay on a sincere compliment and they shine—even the cynical ones who see themselves as benchwarmers in the game of school.

Well, guess what? Teachers are the same. They crave recognition like a dieter craves dessert. But here's the problem. Most educators labor in anonymity for very modest salaries, in the heyday of the rich and famous. They could be bought and sold by recent graduates who proudly announce, "Everything I need to know, I learned on the Internet!" It's not that teachers are totally unappreciated. Some of their students adore them. The occasional parent actually thanks them. But communities as a whole are slow to praise and quick to point the finger when performance drops or test scores disappoint.

Consequently, one of the most pervasive complaints administrators and union leaders hear from teachers is that they don't feel respected or valued for their work. That's where you fit in. Put praise mongering on your To Do list and see how your staff perks up.

Duly Noted

Like most of you, I've attended hundreds of district meetings, and I can count on one hand the number that incorporated *any* principles of good learning. Most were more like a hostage situation, with me vigorously resisting the first signs of Stockholm syndrome.

Budget meetings led by the fiscal gurus were the worst. After forty-five minutes of overheads with numbers so tiny it felt like an eye test, I wanted to stand up and shout, "Would *you* sit still for this?"

The bad news is that most management meetings are boring as hell. The good news is, your hands are free, so I filled the idle hours dashing off encouraging notes to my staff. I kept a stash of stationary in my daybook. Nothing large or expensive. Note cards are perfect because you usually run out of space before you run out of ideas. As the meetings dragged on, I would mentally replay the day, sifting for images of teachers or classes who stood out. Then I'd pen two or three sentences about their achievement. Nothing elaborate. Think Hemingway for this assignment. "It was a good and true assembly. Your preparation made it a success." The point is, people rarely receive praise in writing, so they react as if they'd won the football pool.

Maybe you're thinking, "Easy for you. You're a writer." True, but you don't need Pulitzer material to succeed at this. Just focus on the things you know best—teaching and learning. Be specific about effective strategies you observed, and the quality of the work that students are doing. Use concrete language. Reinforce the behavior you value. Here are some phrases to jump-start the process. Simply modify them for your staff.

Sample Messages

- I saw your class in the library and was so impressed with their enthusiasm for partner reading. Several were devouring a chapter book in the corner. You're a great literacy coach.
- What a great chemistry lesson! I love the way you achieve full student participation in a demonstration lesson. It's your inquiry technique. Bravo! Their lab drawings are detailed and reflect a high level of comprehension.

- The noise level in your room is music to my ears! Every student was engaged and thinking.

- I love the way you answer questions with questions, putting the thinking where it belongs—back in the students' laps.

- Your students are really developing their debating skills. How can we share this with parents and interested staff?

- Broadway lost a star when you chose education. Your read-aloud skills are amazing. No wonder your kids are such avid listeners and readers!

- So this is AP calculus! If I'd had a teacher like you, I might have understood math instead of just grinding out formulas. Well done!

- Thanks for the way you handled the new student who arrived today. You made him seem like a gift to your class instead of an interruption.

- Thanks for being so generous with your technology skills. We'd be lost in cyberspace without you.

- Thank you for helping the new teachers in your department feel welcome. You have excellent mentoring skills. I appreciate your generosity and professionalism. Have you thought about presenting at a leadership conference this year?

- I noticed how you modified your writing assignment to help second-language learners edit their first drafts. It seemed to be helping other students, too. Great work.

- Your lunchtime chess club is a real boon for kids who need companionship, stimulation, and a safe haven. Can I join?

Now you give it a try. Think of a staff member that you really admire. Look at your watch. Write two sentences that capture one talent or habit you appreciate in this person. Look at your watch again. It doesn't take long—maybe two minutes—to get someone's attention. In half an hour you can have a major impact on fifteen people who call you "boss." The trick is to keep it brief. No more than three sentences. It's the thought that counts.

Use a staff roster to keep track of the recipients. Your impulse will be to write twenty times to the brilliant humanist and skip the curmudgeon, so get a system. It never comes out even, and that's not the point. Just make sure everybody gets a boost once in a while. Although it may require some head scratching, I've never met a staff member without some redeeming feature. Looking for it can help you build a stronger relationship with people who may feel overlooked or disenfranchised.

No time for notes? I used to stick Post-it Notes on teachers' desks as I cruised in and out of classrooms. That square inch of praise can mean a lot to a teacher who's casting her pearls before five-year-olds. They love her, but can't appreciate her genius, so when you note that she's teaching phonics using four distinct modalities, you become the hero. You prove that you recognize good teaching and value her efforts—with a Post-it Note!

> *"The deepest principle of human nature is the craving to be appreciated."*
> —William James

Applause! Applause!

Praise is good. Praise with an audience is better. So smart leaders create opportunities to publicly recognize exemplary activities on campus. Here are some examples:

- The science fair had five hundred visitors over the weekend, including the chairman of General Electric. Thanks to the science department for their leadership.
- Our annual Organic Garden Tour will be held next week and record crowds are expected for gardening demonstrations from the botany students in Mr. Smythe's class.
- Five students from Mrs. Mahoney's French class won scholarships to study for six weeks in France.
- Ms. Bartoli's class will have a publishing party and book signing for their local history guide, *Under Any Rock*.

Broadcasting achievements isn't just a feel-good strategy—although it can definitely strengthen esprit de corps. Applause announcements promote collaboration by building a "go-to" network. With a two-line blurb in the staff bulletin, you expose every staff member to a new idea and their local source. The tell-me-more crowd can follow up with email or over lunch. This is a professional development strategy that even the poorest school can afford. Finally, regular Applause items highlight your idea of best practices and reinforce professional standards.

> *"Nine-tenths of education is encouragement."*
> —Anatole France

How to Applaud

- Keep the focus on teaching and learning.
- Describe the effect on students.
- Tell how this activity relates to your vision for all students.
- Spread the recognition around.
- Keep track of who gets applause on a staff roster.

Where to Applaud

- Open your daily or weekly bulletin with words like *Bravo, Congratulations, Well Done, Let's Hear It For,* followed by mention of a special achievement by staff or students.
- Send email announcements to the whole staff.
- Have an Applause column in the PTA bulletin or newsletter.
- Post an Applause note on the refrigerator in the staff lounge.
- Post announcements at the sign-in sheet.
- List an Applause section on every staff-meeting agenda.
- Mount an Applause bulletin board on the door of the faculty lounge.
- Invite, cajole, bribe, or drag board members, the superintendent, community members, and district supervisors into classrooms to show off excellence.
- Develop a symbol, perhaps two hands clapping, that is your Applause logo. Used consistently, it promotes a sense of accomplishment and pride.

Straight from Their Hearts

Have you ever noticed that criticism always travels in the fast lane, while excellence and hard work are about as noteworthy as the grand opening of a strip mall? This ratio of criticism to praise is demoralizing to staff and reduces productivity. Yet surveys tell us that most parents who are discouraged about education in general are satisfied with their neighborhood school. But they rarely say so. They're not ingrates—just very busy. You're in a perfect position to link parents and teachers in a positive dialogue by priming the compliment pump. The next time your parent newsletter goes out, include a Many Thanks form. Make it user-friendly and to the point—like this:

MANY THANKS

TO: _____

FROM: _____

We just wanted to let you know how much we appreciate you as a teacher.

We really like

_____

_____

_____

Keep up the good work.

Yes, it's a form. But it's a first step in building a culture of appreciation, by gently reminding parents that teachers deserve praise. And it's so easy that many parents take the hint. The comments section gives teachers specific feedback on what parents value and begins to change the perception of parents as insatiable malcontents.

Honorable Mention

Parents often rave about their kids' teachers at a PTA meeting or in your office, but what's the good of compliments if teachers never hear them? When parents drool over the International Bread Festival in Room 10, or praise the science teacher who organized the beach cleanup, scoop up those compliments and express-mail them to the rightful owner. The Honorable Mention form takes about thirty seconds of your time, but it is a very powerful tool for building bridges between parents and a wary staff. It can make a teacher's whole day or week worthwhile—and this is one time when they won't want to kill the messenger!

HONORABLE MENTION

_____

You were mentioned by

_____

because _____

_____

Thank you for your fine work.

Relationships

Every September, new teachers arrive at schools so congested that teachers can't bribe their way into the parking lot. The halls are teeming with bodies, the front office resembles the trading floor of the New York Stock Exchange, and they don't know a soul. Their first and only friend may be the custodian.

We all know that teaching can be lonely work. Novices may never meet exemplary teachers because they're in a different building or their departments are at war. Talented but eccentric veterans ignore newcomers and peers alike from the splendid isolation of their rooms. Everybody loses if you don't figure out a way to nurture personal and professional relationships on your staff. And don't kid yourself. A faculty meeting is not a social venue.

Getting to Know You

It can take years for colleagues sharing the same campus to discover that they have more in common than bad timing at the cafeteria and Xerox lines. People need more than an ID badge and a passing nod to go on. They need information. The simplest way to link people on your staff is to include short biographies in your bulletins. They're guaranteed to boost readership since most of us love details about other people. Not gossip per se, but definitely intriguing tidbits.

How can you gather the information? Design a simple form or questionnaire. Ask about hobbies, graduate degrees, languages spoken, favorite author, favorite vacation destination, latest accomplishment, current challenge, wishes, hopes, and dreams. Include a few unusual questions—What's the best birthday celebration your every had? Who's your hero? Have staff spend a few minutes filling out the forms during a staff meeting at the beginning of the school year.

When you're poised to write these bios, choose a new teacher and a veteran. Relate five to seven facts about each. Keep the writing brief. Interested readers will fill in the blanks. Publish these profiles regularly until the whole staff has been introduced—including support staff and administrators.

Connecting

Management by wandering has a lot of virtues. One is that you're in a perfect position to discover connections between disparate parts of the campus. As you visit classrooms, make notes about curriculum, projects, discussion topics, or upcoming events. Then share that information with classes or staff working in the same vein to encourage collaboration. You become the intersection where ideas meet and projects are hatched. File away information about individuals' skills. Then the next time someone has a computer meltdown in the middle of a project, you can connect them with the teacher who can hotwire a mainframe. Another way to connect staff members is choosing like-minded strangers to work on a project together, so they get acquainted. Lifelong friendships, even marriages, have started this way.

Offers and Requests

Picture e-bay on campus, but instead of exchanging vintage cameras or Thomas Jefferson memorabilia, your staff swaps professional and curricular services and opportunities. Here's how it works. Teachers use email, the weekly bulletin, or a notice board to post offers and requests. For example:

> **Offer:** Have three journalism students who will write a short piece about life in your classroom for the school paper. Deadline January 14. Contact Sue R.

> **Request:** Am doing water measuring experiments with class on Monday. Need as many buckets as possible from 9–11. Anne B.

Offer: My students are presenting their final projects on the Middle Ages. Need interested audience armed with good questions for interactive experience. Call for reservations. Michelle, ext. 234.

Request: Would love to watch someone teach the coediting section of writer's workshop. My kids aren't getting it. Call John at ext. 391.

Don't just encourage this professional swap meet—roll up your sleeves and make it happen. Volunteer to cover that teacher's class while he goes to watch a writer's workshop. Pretty soon the word will be out. The principal can do *and* teach. Your stock will rise.

Resources

No one signs on to teaching for the perks. No one brags about the plush facilities or fat paychecks. In fact, teaching is largely a triumph of ingenuity over scarcity. But as the administrator, you do have some resources at your disposal. Use them to encourage and motivate staff. Here's a short list of materials and opportunities your can spread around to spread good cheer.

- Snag a new video that just came into the library and deliver it to a classroom that is studying a related topic.
- Send teams of teachers to high-quality conferences related to your vision, and have them teach the rest of the staff when they return. If your budget is slim, contact your county office of education for free professional development opportunities. Ask your PTA to devote part of their budget each year to staff development. Identify community resources, such as the police or fire department to conduct school safety trainings.
- Ask the local art museum if you can bring your staff for a meeting and walk-through.
- Pass on invitations to art openings, seminars, or free concerts that you can't attend.
- Lend your professional books to teachers for their own research and growth.
- Xerox your notes from interesting meetings that you attend and pass them along to appropriate staff members.
- Pass on professional bulletins after you read them.
- Direct teachers to websites related to their curriculum.

- Connect classes with community resources such as a local historian, university staff, artists, architects, writers, scientists, or merchants.
- Facilitate field trips using local resources and the public bus.

Rewards

If you think little things don't mean a lot, put a Snickers Bar in every teacher's box and watch the stampede. I discovered the power of chocolate early in my administrative career. On rainy days, Fridays, faculty meeting days, or any time morale—theirs or mine—seemed to dip, I'd lob a chunk of chocolate into every mailbox. And inevitably, the mood would brighten. Two pounds of sweets bought a lot of good will!

You may think this sounds patronizing—like doing trick-or-treat for your staff. Would you believe it's one of the techniques suggested by Debra Harris in *What Counts: How Forward-Thinking Leaders Recognize and Reward Employees* (2000)? You have to decide what fits your style. All I can tell you is that the reaction to the tasty apparitions was always the same. Delight. Requests for more. Why are grown-ups tickled by the sight of a six-cent hunk of carbohydrates? The obvious explanation—it was unexpected. Everybody likes surprises. Plus, it lets them know I am thinking about them. But I think the most compelling explanation is that teachers work in an environment of unrelenting scarcity. Hoarding is a survival tool. Scrounging and recycling are right up there with behavior-management skills. Many teachers routinely stock and furnish their classrooms at their own expense. So any gesture, however small, is appreciated.

I branched out from chocolate, discovering dozens of no-cost and low-cost ways to reward the staff and let them know that I appreciated their efforts.

Here's a list of my favorites, in no special order.

- Stop at intervals during extra long staff meetings to raffle off plants, coffee coupons, or movie passes.
- Convince a local restaurant to give 10 percent off discount cards to staff.
- Give gift certificates for latte to the first three people who turn in their monthly reports.
- Ask a local bookstore to donate seconds to the library in the staff lounge.
- Order a subscription to an interesting newspaper for the staff lunchroom.

- Supply healthy snacks during parent conferences.
- Give compliments—they're free and they lift spirits.
- Offer coupons worth one recess or lunch supervision duty—you're the stand-in.
- Offer to be a guest lecturer in a class you'd like to teach.
- Organize a staff retreat at a local home, park, hotel, community center, or business conference room.
- Hold a raffle for staff who turn in grades/report cards on time.
- Put a bouquet of flowers at the sign-in sheet and send them home with a raffle winner in the afternoon.

Rituals

Rituals mark the passage of time, and slowly knit individuals into a community. Repeated celebrations, with new faces among the old, create a sense of family among colleagues. Start your own celebratory rituals that take advantage of the cyclical nature of the school year, and soon people will look forward to them as a tradition. For a start, plan events at traditional holidays—Thanksgiving, first day of spring, winter solstice, winter break, Valentine's Day, St. Patrick's Day, or local observances. Tap into the psychological power of these holidays—a positive mood, nostalgia, and memories—to increase the staff's pleasure and to bond them to each other and you.

My favorite ritual was planning and hosting a holiday breakfast for the staff. On the last morning before we all left for winter break, my assistant principal and I would do breakfast for the entire staff. First we would transform the lounge with baskets of greenery, tablecloths, candles, and music. Tables were heaped with trays of pastries, wheels of cheese, fruit, and bread. When the staff arrived, the coffee was piping and so were the carols. The festive mood lasted all day, as people wandered in and out for one more scone.

Here are some other starting points for building rituals for your staff and their families.

- Give flowers for special accomplishments.
- Send cards for birthdays.
- Bring healthy snacks during parent conference week.
- Give each teacher a journal at the beginning of the year and start every staff meeting with a prompt and time for reflective writing.
- Start staff meetings by reading a paragraph or poem. Play music as staff arrive. Have food—always food. But you don't have to do it all

yourself. Grade levels or departments can take charge of the various assignments.

- Organize a faculty barbeque or a family picnic.
- Calendar student-faculty softball games.
- Host dinner parties for staff and significant others.

What Gets Rewarded Gets Done

By diligently practicing the five Rs—recognition, relationships, resources, rewards, and rituals—you gently focus your staff's attention on the things you value by valuing the things they do. In addition, you get to have the fun of lifting morale and strengthening the personal and professional network at your school. Train yourself to prospect for every opportunity to be a positive model. With a little effort, you can go down in history as a great principal, and a remarkable Fezziwig.

7

Do Nothing for Staff That They Can Do for Themselves

Getting Smarter About Distributing Leadership

- Project Thinking: Retooling Your View of Leadership
- The Seedbed: Identifying Potential Projects
- The Greenhouse: Restructuring for Project Work
- Group Gardening: Organizing Meetings to Promote Projects
- Power Gardening: Putting Projects in Overdrive
- Weeds in the Project Garden: Dealing with Obstacles

One of the great paradoxes of education is that we entrust teachers with our most precious resource, then turn around and treat them like parolees or overgrown children. We abandon them to teach unevaluated for years but won't let them into the supply closet without an escort. If we're long on kids and short on texts, we post an armed guard at the book room.

Clock-watching administrators pore over sign-in sheets like bank examiners but never set foot in classrooms. Bells signal the outer limits of lessons, with no opportunity for a passionate instructor to say, "Ignore that—we're knee-deep in covalent bonding!" Charged with making a thousand educational decisions for kids, teachers are rarely asked to design their own professional development programs.

In short, we in the business of education routinely underestimate our greatest potential asset—the teaching force. If you think I'm exaggerating, just treat yourself to a typical staff meeting—the nadir of school management.

Staff meetings are painful rituals that underscore the Mother-may-I culture of schools. Teachers who have spent their day orchestrating complex academic and social interactions are

suddenly treated like the dump class—not too bright and potentially unruly. The administrator—in full body armor—warily
presides, one eye on a predictable agenda, the other on an unpre-
dictable crowd. Participation is optional. The group norm—
Endure, and then we can get out of here!

Which is not to say that nothing gets done during these affairs.
Hundreds of papers are corrected. Essays are edited; tests scored and
grades recorded; newspapers read; daybooks updated; birthday
cards circulated; stocks checked on palm pilots; vacations planned;
thank-you notes penned; and checkbooks balanced. Occasionally, a
discreet nap. It's like a study hall for teachers, with a pesky but
largely ineffective administrator trying to attract their attention.

Scanning the audience you'll see a sprinkling of catatonics
and seditionists, clustered in job-alike groups or huddled together
for protection. The list of other characters is fairly predictable.

- Industrious Captives arrive with bulging Lands' End tote-
  bags, intent on plowing through their appointed tasks while
  ignoring the background noise provided by the agenda.
- Designated Whiners are as predictable as television com-
  mercials, and just about as much fun. The minute they start
  in, eyes roll. Everyone knows their portfolio of complaints,
  and no one cares.
- Predators are on alert for any chink in the administrative
  armor. Some are content to snipe. Others launch a full
  frontal attack.
- Hijackers seize an agenda item, mount it as if it were a
  soapbox, and shoot from the lip. They fire questions, pass
  out documents constructed in secret, and generally domi-
  nate the room.

It can take a quarter of an hour to get the meeting back on track
after one of these outbursts. Sometimes it's a dead loss. Meanwhile, the majority of the staff sits in silence, hoping you'll win this
not-so-subtle tug-of-war.

Everyone watches the clock.

This is not fertile territory for gardening. Sensitive people get
agitated or shut down to shield themselves from the negative vibes.
Others attend just to see the show. In some schools, up to a third
of the staff is routinely AWOL, despite the contract language. If
most principals had their way, they'd be AWOL, too.

But as the principal, you *do* have some choices. Here's one. Stop wasting everyone's time in fruitless meetings. Reorganize the work of the school into projects, so that staff members address all issues that don't require your personal stewardship. You can turn a minefield the size of Yankee Stadium into a fertile plot and watch it grow and bloom from one season to the next, simply by reorganizing the work of your school into projects.

Project Thinking: Retooling Your View of Leadership

Think of projects as group gardening. Staff members select the plot of their choice, organize their work, enlist aid from colleagues or experts when necessary, and share the bounty of their labor to benefit the whole school community. Projects are problem-solving structures wherein teams of adults work together to share the responsibility for student success.

If that sounds like just another word for a committee, think again. Committee is a leaden word. It has the taint of showing up and sticking it out as the criteria for success. No new thinking is demanded when people sign up for committee membership.

By contrast, projects are about building. They address concrete tasks connected to teachers' work with their students. They are goal driven and time limited, with a fair amount of trial and error guided by research and staff expertise. They meet as needed, publish their work, report out at faculty meetings, and use the whole group as a resource for input, brainstorming, feedback, and refinements. When the desired product or condition is achieved, the project team celebrates, dissolves, and moves on.

The Power of Project Thinking

Projects assert that teachers are the rightful decision makers in matters of policy and practice about students because of their expertise. As the ultimate on-the-grounders they deserve to have a true voice in the school, which means they also earn the accompanying responsibility to move from words to action. Projects hold staff directly responsible for making progress toward collective goals, and their collaborative work has meaning for the whole community.

> *"You cannot help men permanently by doing for them what they could and should do for themselves."*
>
> —Abraham Lincoln

This may sound like a lot of work for staff, but research suggests that when teachers are empowered, morale improves. Projects trumpet your expectations for the staff—professional development, collegiality, autonomy, and open communication. They also send a strong message about you as a leader. Promoting project thinking startles staffs who are used to the upstairs/downstairs approach to school administration. It's unconventional and counternormative. You model behavior that deviates from the status quo, behavior you hope staff will adopt with each other and with their students. It looks risky or self-sacrificing to apparently give away the scant amount of power that you have. It sends a message to staff that you are committed to distributing leadership.

The first shift in restructuring for project work has to happen inside your head. Business as usual will get you just that. So get tough with yourself. Confront anything in your calendar that's an empty ritual. Make every meeting and memo justify itself. If it doesn't contribute to the work of the school, dump it.

- A prime suspect needs to be announcements. If you make fifteen minutes of announcements to forty people, you've used up ten hours of human productivity—probably on items that most people will ignore or forget. Remind yourself every day that you're dealing with a population of literate professionals. Do nothing at meetings that can be done via bulletins, email, or memos. Banning nuts-and-bolts items from meetings frees up valuable time for staff collaboration on projects.
- Publish your bulletin—electronically and on paper—on a specific day. Staff can read notices at their leisure, or download them to put them in their planbook or palm pilot. They'll become regular, if not devoted, readers when they realize it's the only source for useful information. Don't review bulletin material at whole-group meetings. If asked, refer to the published source.
- Organize all staff work into projects. Staff meetings become project time.

The Seedbed: Identifying Potential Projects

Where are projects found? In casual conversations, over lunch, in the suggestion box, at parent meetings, even in complaints. In fact, think of complainers as project consultants without the hefty fees. The school community is one big seedbed from which you can pluck an issue and start growing a project. Here's a list of sample projects:

- Revise the 504 process, including parent surveys, forms, and tracking systems.

- Develop an interdepartment seminar on reading strategies for older nonreaders.
- Build a mainstreaming protocol for training teachers and aides who serve fully included students.
- Create a fine arts program in all grades K–5.
- Write a parent education module to improve parent and teacher satisfaction during parent conferences.
- Reconfigure the school week to build project time into the day.
- Develop an apprenticeship program to parallel AP classes.
- Investigate authentic assessment as an alternative to tests in selected classes.
- Merge history and English classes to form humanities blocks.
- Create a Peace Academy to train students in nonviolence and conflict resolution.
- Create a grant-writing support group.
- Form a National Board Certification cohort.

Identifying potential projects should be easy for most principals, since they work on projects all the time. The trouble is that most principals are experts at doing projects alone. If a delegation of two insists that the parent conference format "no longer reflects the goals of the school," you could spend the weekend hammering out a solution. On Monday, it's shot down in a hail of critical remarks about the half-dozen flaws that make it entirely unworkable and the "autocratic administrators who never consult staff." Bottom line? Nobody likes your solution.

But if you had viewed that complaint as the starting point for a project, you would have published the concern, set up a clearinghouse for suggestions, and spent the weekend in relative leisure. One of the following would have happened. You would never hear about this issue again; some people would make suggestions that the majority would reject; or a group would adopt the complaints as a project, and they'd be off and running. After all, they're the ones who have to conduct conferences. They have a vested interest in getting it right.

The Greenhouse: Restructuring for Project Work

When the work of the school is reorganized into staff-driven projects, does life get easier for you? Yes and no. Without projects, you try to respond to every issue that crops up, relegating yourself to the position of a well-paid handyman

> "Getting things done is not always what is important. There is value in allowing others to learn, even if the task is not accomplished as quickly, efficiently or effectively."
>
> —R. D. Clyde

for the staff—the fix-it principal. By assuming that teachers should do the creative decision-making work of the school, you can give up the role of the busybody, in-box manager.

You won't be idle. You will still have projects of your own, but the bulk of your time will be spent tending to a half dozen or more greenhouses, where you're growing new leaders for the school. Greenhouses are controlled environments where teachers develop leadership skills as they grapple with ways to ensure student success. As head gardener, you're responsible for watering, feeding, and temperature control. At project meetings, you coach committed self-starters on group-process skills and encourage reluctant participants.

To boost the chances of success, give all project leaders a strategic thinking template for moving their projects from idea to execution.

A Basic Outline for Project Work

1. What is the goal of the project?
2. How does it address the educational birthright of all students?
3. What are the specific benefits for students?
4. Who might share your interest in achieving this goal?
5. How can you enlist their participation?
6. How can you get constructive input from people who might oppose your plans?
7. What administrative support will you need?
8. At what point do you need to share with the full staff?
9. How long will it take to achieve the goal?
10. When will you begin and end?
11. What are the specific tasks necessary to achieve the goal? List in chronological order.
12. How will you know when you have accomplished your goal?

You may need to support the project teams by clearing away bureaucratic debris that hinders their work or offering to locate resources or information. Throughout you will need to monitor their progress, but most of all you will share responsibility, distribute leadership, and model skills that promote autonomy. When teams are ready to bring their project to the whole group, you provide moral support and temperature control.

Group Gardening: Organizing Meetings to Promote Projects

Project leaders may do a bang-up job galvanizing a small group of like-minded colleagues, but shake in their boots at the thought of presenting their ideas to the whole faculty— and worse, asking for input. It's your job to create a safe way for novice leaders to practice group-process skills and gain confidence.

> *"It is the responsibility of leadership to provide opportunities, and the responsibility of individuals to contribute."*
>
> —Bill Polland

Happily, you have the element of surprise on your side. People are so used to flat-lining at staff meetings that they're shocked at the notion of having a productive, even stimulating, encounter with their peers. They may emerge from a peppy meeting with new respect for themselves and their colleagues. Well-run, project-centered meetings can accomplish that and more. They also build organizational morale by generating evidence of group intelligence and efficacy. Collegiality increases as the staff learns to support one another through meaningful work.

The following steps will set up teacher-leaders for success as they facilitate project work at whole-staff meetings.

1. Start with clear agenda items submitted by project leaders and published in advance. Include a precis that indicates the amount of group time allotted to each agenda item, the goal of the work, formats or activities, and what is expected of all participants, including any preparation needed for the meeting.

2. Each time a project is agendized it will be to update the whole staff on progress toward goals, get input for next steps, check for effectiveness, or fine-tune the product.

3. Organize the agenda for success. Put an easy item first, perhaps an update on a project that is going well, to set a positive tone. Put the hardest work in the middle. Save a moderately interesting but noncontroversial issue for last, so that the meeting ends on a productive but harmonious note.

4. Use premeeting strategies to promote cooperation and discourage sabotage. Meet with project heads to review formats and desired outcomes. Touch base with negative or needy staffers. Give them a little extra attention right before the meeting, and listen for hidden agendas, bones of contention, or potential derails.

5. Use room logistics to promote success. Never hold a meeting in a messy room. It depresses morale and shouts disorganization, carelessness, or sloth. If nothing else, straighten all the chairs, and hit a few tables with a liquid cleaner so it smells fresh. Organize the furniture to aid the process—circles of chairs, tables for small-group work, easels for recording. Sometimes it pays to shift furniture just to change expectations. Have a "Look at This!" table at the entrance to the room. Instead of the usual handouts, feature new books or videos purchased by the library, professional or technical magazines to borrow, pamphlets from local cultural institutions, announcements of art openings, and posters from the science museum. Make the table attractive. A vase of flowers or a cutaway model of the brain will jolt a few synapses, and that's a good way to start any meeting.

6. Change meeting locations. Gather in the room of the presenters or take a tour of a project site. If the playfields are on the agenda, meet at the bleachers and have a discussion in three dimensions. If you have a small faculty, rotate meetings from room to room so staff can observe room environments and get lesson ideas as value added to the meeting.

7. Group norms. Have the group construct and agree on norms at the beginning of the school year. If they don't seem to work, revisit them as often as necessary until you get the deportment you need. Chart your norms and post them at every meeting, Write them at the top of every agenda. Some sample norms:

   - one conversation at a time
   - watch your air time
   - constructive dialogue, no put-downs
   - hard on issues, soft on people
   - no process without a product

People are less likely to violate norms when their peers are running the meeting. But if they do, your role is to challenge the scofflaws. Their compliance may be grudging, but insisting on it shows you are serious about the work.

8. Write the start and finish times on the agenda and stick to them religiously. People are more willing to commit their energy to a group process if they can count on it ending punctually. Ending five minutes early is even better.

9. Have the goals of the meeting posted on a chart as well as on the agenda.

10. Have multiple white boards or easels set up for recording ideas and outcomes. Suggest that the recorders use two or three bright colors to code ideas. Charts create a visible group memory and can be reintroduced at subsequent meetings as primary source documents. Charts also depersonalize ideas. Instead of finding fault with a person, participants can say, "I think there might be a problem with #3 on that chart."

11. Label one chart For Future Consideration. This is the place for valuable comments or ideas that emerge during the discussion but don't fit in the current conversation.

12. Charts keep the meeting on course by outlining the steps of the process, and recording progress. This is especially useful if you have staffers who can't find their "off" button, or feel they haven't been heard. Operating under the notion that if they just say it one more time, the group will understand, they repeat themselves, give too many details, and wear everyone out. Pointing to their ideas on the chart acknowledges that they are already on the record.

13. Use body language to encourage participation. Be attentive to the person who is speaking. Nod, smile, lean forward, and make eye contact.

14. End with enough time to review progress and discuss next steps.

15. Limit the number and length of whole-group project meetings. Cancel any scheduled meetings that become unnecessary, even if you have to do it at the last minute. It shows respect for people's time and makes actual meetings all the more important.

Power Gardening: Putting Projects in Overdrive

Projects, like gardens, need a lot of tending, especially in the early stages, before they put down roots and really begin to grow. Typically projects get stuck when the weight of the problems is greater than the energy or creativity of the working group. That's the time to get all hands on deck. The more brain power the better. But unfocused input can be crushing—worse than none at all. Two formats that can generate direction and speed for faltering projects are Imagine a Different Reality and Force-Field Analysis. Project members can use these tools to clarify their own work, or to interact with a larger group—community, parents, or the whole staff—to brainstorm dozens of ideas for potential action, to gather input on a particular problem, to bring opposition out in the open, to determine next steps, or to fine-tune a product.

Format 1: Imagine a Different Reality

The first focus group format, Imagine a Different Reality, is a powerful way to acknowledge the worst aspects of an issue and use them as a springboard for imagining a superior reality. The format is so simple that almost anyone can facilitate, with large groups or small. It's so honest that even the most disgruntled participant feels heard, and so constructive that people feel uplifted by their work and progress.

The process has three parts:

1. Identify concerns about the current situation.
2. Organize the concerns into categories or themes.
3. Imagine and describe a new reality in which those concerns have been addressed.

I used this format with parents, teachers, and administrators when our department was trapped in special education hell. It seemed we had two choices—get out and talk to people or huddle in our offices and wait for incoming fire—irate phone calls, faxes from lawyers, and a small army of investigators from the Office of Civil Rights. Talking worked.

I opened each session by thanking the group for taking time to help us imagine a new reality in special education. I explained that in order to get to that point, we needed to identify concerns in the current program. Then I announced, "I'll go first!" I had already printed on index cards the top-ten complaints we heard over and over—phone calls not returned, high staff turnover, insufficient number of specialists, regular education teachers who knew little and cared less about accommodations, emergency credentials in critical staffing positions, insufficient recruitment, adversarial IEP meetings, and the list went on.

As I read each problem, I pinned it to a bulletin board for all to see. The participants were surprised to hear me volunteer our darkest sins, surprised that this session would be about truth telling, and visibly relieved that I had done the heaviest lifting for them.

Then I invited the audience to "tell me more." I wrote each concern on a card and stuck it randomly on the board until all the ideas were on display. No matter how harsh the criticism, I wrote it without flinching. Accepting their remarks encouraged participation. Then I sat down with the group and we stared at the data. It was not a pretty sight.

Next I asked the group to get up and reorganize the cards into categories. There was a lot of discussion, debate, and interaction, which made a good break after a spell of nervous sitting. Some of the categories they created were communication, staff development, service delivery, and parent education.

Once the categories were complete, I asked participants to imagine a different reality—one in which we had a world-class special education program. I recorded all their suggestions by category on large charts. As a final step we identified the three improvements in each category that were the most urgent.

Sessions like this stir emotions, so you may want to go once around the circle and have each person make one final comment. Mine was always a sincere thanks for their time and intelligence.

Using this format, we were able to collect huge amounts of direct input from diverse groups all around the district. It was synthesized, presented to the board, and translated into an action plan. We also reaped a bumper crop of goodwill. Many of the focus sessions ended with hugs, expressions of gratitude, and a couple of "you're so brave to do this." I recommend this format when you need to get lots of people involved in problem solving around the thorniest issues.

Format 2: Force-Field Analysis

Force-Field Analysis is a very efficient strategy for clarifying a problem, identifying obstacles, and zeroing in on solutions. It is effective for members of a small work group to structure their efforts or for the entire staff. It breaks down into seven steps.

1. Focus on a situation that needs changing—the reason for the project. Describe as specifically as possible the problematic traits of the situation.

2. Fast-forward five years. What will the situation be like without any interventions?

3. Think about what the ideal situation would be if interventions were applied.

4. Identify what could cause that change and what is standing in the way.

5. Brainstorm ways to remove or minimize the obstacles.

6. Identify a sequence of steps to get from the current state to the desired state.

7. Sketch out a time line and divide up the tasks.

Weeds in the Project Garden: Dealing with Obstacles

Project work is stimulating and rewarding, but it requires generous amounts of quality time, which is rarely in abundance at school sites. Good teachers guard the precious hours they have with their students—as well they should. Some even refuse to take roll or make announcements because it cuts into instructional minutes! So subbing teachers out may not be popular. And prep time should be used for good solid instructional preparation. So when do they work on projects? They can't do groundbreaking work in five-minute increments over the drone of the Xerox machine, and after school everyone is exhausted.

Finding time is an important part of your job—a way to fertilize the garden. Safeguarding staff meetings for cooperative endeavors is an essential first step. Here are some other ways you can buy time for project work:

- Sub out team members and have a guest teacher or presentation for their students.
- Take on several classes yourself for special student-principal dialogues.
- Arrange schedules so that team members have prep periods at the same time.
- Bank time if the contract allows. Extend each day for ten to fifteen minutes then have students start late or end the day early once a week for staff work.
- If your budget can bear it, send whole teams to professional development training related directly to their project.
- Look to the business or philanthropic community for underwriting, and think about tapping resources in the corporate world for specialized training, or import high-impact trainers who have excellent reputations.
- Sponsor a monthly breakfast for project groups. You supply the coffee and bagels an hour before school starts. They come and work together. It's an invigorating way to start the day.

Fuzzy Roles

A critical element in any plan to distribute leadership is clarity about who's doing what. Don't waste precious time with fuzziness. Expect staff to make all the decisions they can, and be very clear about the decisions you will retain. If revamping the teacher evaluation process is a site prerogative, turn them loose on it. If it's written in contract cement let that be known and move on to more fertile topics. If you introduce a topic for group discussion, tell the staff why—to prospect for ideas, to fine-tune an existing plan, or to make a decision by vote or consensus. If you need a specific outcome—such as closing the library to gain a classroom, don't bother with group process, hoping to engineer a victory. Tell the staff what you've decided, and then spend the time working on solutions to the problems that may arise.

Sharing Power

Union representatives can be instrumental in promoting project work. They may have several topics that they want to address in a project format. It is also possible that they may try to undermine project work because it blurs the line between labor and management. As teacher-leaders move from isolation to participation, they become part of the power structure, working alongside administrators rather than under them. When teachers lead, they discover ways to control their work and working conditions, often without the need for union mediation.

Recognizing this, hard-liners may join projects in pairs or threes if they see them as threatening traditional union positions. By joining en masse, they can maintain control and block the changes that they oppose.

What to do? Send teams of novice and senior teachers to professional development sessions together. Ask union representatives to train your whole group in something that they know or do well. Build their status as a resource to the school. Praise them in public. Find pieces of their agenda that intersect with project work and build a project around them.

Toxic Behavior

In every walk of life, every large gathering, there are a few individuals who are truly rabid with dissatisfaction. They assess and condemn everything in their line of vision, including project work. These people have a very negative relationship with life in general—you're just part of the landscape on which they cast their jaundiced eyes. But people with this toxic potential are very few in number. Over time, as your staff grasps the satisfaction of project life, the toxics become more marginalized and isolated. They will never be pleasant to deal with, but their power will diminish. Eventually they may abandon the garden for browner pastures.

Sticking with It

Abandoning the authoritarian command-and-control style of leadership and enlisting the cooperation, involvement, and self-actualizing potential of all employees provides excitement, but also a new set of challenges. Everybody has to become a learner. Don't expect support for projects and distributed leadership to be universal. Young teachers may embrace project work more readily than veterans, causing friction in schools where seasoned teachers have done things their way for so long that they rule by inertia.

> "A leader is best when people barely know he exists. When his work is done, his aim fulfilled, they will say: We did it ourselves."
>
> —Lao-Tzu

Enthusiastic reformers may run straight into the teeth of antiquated policies or cautious board members, and you'll need all your skills to stand behind your staff and stand up to your boss. Sparks will fly in a hundred different directions. Step back and enjoy the light show. Don't expect everyone to get project fever the first month, or even the first year. Some people will seize the opportunity to lead. Others will hang back or disappear. Don't worry. Don't go for the 100 percent solution. This is culture change, so give it plenty of time. Eventually, most staffers will understand that projects give them tools and power. They learn to garden and like it.

8

Where the Rubber Meets the Road

Getting Smarter About Supervising Instruction

- Now Hear This: Broadcasting Your Intentions
- Breaking Away: Reserving Time for Classroom Visits
- Covering the Territory: Organizing Focused Visits
- Digging In: Investigating Teaching and Learning
- Promoting Your Vision: Publicizing Your Observations
- Gauging Your Impact: Responding to Staff Reactions

Good principals work very hard, every day, at dozens of dull, thankless tasks. They soldier through the week, from budget crises to suspensions, with an ironclad guarantee that there's more where that came from. Entire days may go by without ever setting foot in the true center of power—the classrooms.

Why? Because visiting classrooms just puts you several hours and thirty-seven emails behind in your perpetual struggle against that-which-must-be-done. It may even feel faintly indulgent—like a little holiday—to flee the morass of managerial tasks for the familiar turf of the classroom. Suddenly you feel energized. You feel effective—this is what principals are supposed to do! You remember what's great about your school—and your job.

So demand your right to be where the action is—in the garden, with the kids. Classroom visits are, after all, the essence of gardening in the minefield—the only way to witness the tilling, planting, growth, bounty, and sometimes a crop failure.

Regular, purposeful visits are the most direct way to improve learning for all kids because they send a message that you feel personally responsible for student achievement, and that you will actively contribute your knowledge to shaping instruction, not just evaluating teachers. You belong in classrooms every day. I don't mean poke your head in, compliment a bulletin board, and move

84

on. And those mandatory overrehearsed observations prescribed by the teachers' contract definitely don't count. You need to be willfully and persistently curious about what's going on in every room.

A System for Success

Once you decide to make the switch from office prisoner to high-visibility gardener, the obstacles will multiply. You'll head for the chemistry lab and never make it. Instead, you'll spend forty-five minutes playing human bumper car, careening from one doorway to another, answering questions, taking requests, and completely losing your focus.

Even if you do make it down the hallway, it's unlikely you'll find a welcome mat outside every classroom. In some cases, DO NOT DISTURB is writ large—the door is locked, the transom's sealed, and paper is taped over the observation window. Your instinct will be to sprint past as if the room were radioactive, or head back to the office and forget the whole idea. You will need the strategies discussed in this chapter to sustain your commitment.

Now Hear This: Broadcasting Your Intentions

In some schools, classroom visits are so rare that they fall somewhere between ancient history and mythology. So publicize your plan in advance. Tell your staff, community, peers, and mentor where you'll be spending your time and why.

Tell teachers you'll be visiting regularly to observe teaching and learning, look at student work, and ask kids to explain what they're doing—in short, to participate in the educational process. Let them know that since you're there to see the work, you want them to carry on whenever you arrive. There's no need to stop and ask, "Can I help you?" or prod reluctant students into a singsong "Good morning, Ms. Schmidt."

Tell your administrative staff where you are going and why. You don't want them to feel abandoned in the office with nothing but phone calls and grumpy parents. And you really don't want them to undermine your work by telling callers "I have no idea when she'll be in," which could sound like you're still at home shuffling around in slippers and a robe. Ask staff to tell everyone who calls for you during that time that you're observing in classrooms. When you head out for the classrooms, agree that the office can reach you with a bell signal, by beeper, or by phone, but only if it's very important. And throughout the year, take your office staff with you on classroom visits, so they can see the importance of the work they do to support teachers.

In your newsletter and at every parent meeting, explain the principal's role in supervision. Help the community understand that you are the primary quality-control device in the school, so if they want excellent instruction, they'll need to understand why you don't pick up your own phone when they call. You're in the field, where you belong.

Finally, tell another principal about your visiting schedule, and ask that person to check in with you to see how you're doing. My principal-chum, Wendy Wax, was my partner in this effort. Talking frequently about ways to break the grip of paperwork helped both of us get to the kids more often, though never as much as we wanted. Tell your mentor and your supervisor, then take them along on observations with you. Broadcasting your intentions puts pressure on you to keep up the effort.

Breaking Away: Reserving Time for Classroom Visits

Some days it will take a surprise fire drill to get you out of your office. Every time you come up for air, there's someone else who needs you. Don't assume that you can squeeze a few spontaneous classroom visits in between the dozens of meetings you schedule each week. It simply won't work. So reverse the process. Give kids first dibs on your palm pilot or daybook. Sit down on the first of the month and block out one or more hours each day for visits. I use a yellow highlighter to fill in the whole-classroom observation space, so I can't erase or move it. If you work better in larger chunks, cross off two or three mornings or afternoons per week. Then make a pact with yourself that you'll show up. You wouldn't stand up the superintendent, or a board member, so don't bail out on your kids. Post your classroom visitation schedule on your door. Give it to your office staff. Tell everyone it's Priority One.

If you find your resolve seeping away, picture the students in those rooms who look up to you, are excited by your attention, or sadly, just feel safe when you're in the room. Think about the great teachers who rarely have another adult to witness their brilliance. Personalizing the reason for your visits is more motivating than harping at yourself about being responsible for the quality of education on campus.

Covering the Territory: Organizing Focused Visits

I decided to turn my classroom visits into mini-laboratories so that on every outing I could get smarter about life on my campus. If your school has more than a dozen rooms, you need a system to ensure that you visit all rooms over a period of time. Here are six ways you can organize your observations to fully explore the garden that is your school.

Observe by Grade Level

Parents are ingenious in their ability to do reconnaissance on any grade level that interests them—usually the one to which their child is assigned. They volunteer in rooms, watch from a distance, do informal polling, and request formal visits. There's nothing wrong with that, but they shouldn't know more about the first-grade reading program or honors English than you do. So get into those rooms and arm yourself with information.

On the surface, observing by grade level seems to be comparing apples to apples. In fact, it usually runs the gamut from bananas to pomegranates. You'll get a panoramic view of instruction and details about individual teachers that will help you plan professional development for grade-level teams, identify mentors, and praise expert teachers.

Observe by Subject

To observe by subject, you need to know who's teaching what and when. In an elementary school, it can take a bit of investigating to discover that, but it's well worth your time. The simple act of asking your staff to identify approximate times when they teach various subjects sends a message that you expect those subjects to be taught. It's unfortunate but true, that some teachers routinely "run out of time" or simply skip topics they dislike. If your inquiries send a nervous ripple through the staff, that's a good place to look close, ask questions, and plan staff development.

Suppose you decide to observe science instruction throughout the school. Do a brief review of the existing curriculum. Block out time in your daybook for classroom visits, then go, sit, and take notes. After a few weeks of collecting data, you're in an excellent place to start thinking about the effectiveness of your program. Specifically, you can begin to ask questions such as:

- What themes run from kindergarten through fifth/sixth grade?
- How are children engaged in discovery?
- How do children document their thinking and learning?
- When and how is the scientific method introduced?
- How is science integrated with other disciplines?
- Does the curriculum overlap from grade to grade in ways that help students extend their understanding or just review familiar material?
- Which teachers are exemplary science teachers?
- Who can function as science mentors?

In a middle or high school, the master schedule provides your plan of action. Review the curriculum of each course briefly, pick a certain number of classes per day, observe, and make detailed notes. Meet with the department to give positive feedback and pose questions for mutual investigation.

Observe by Program

There are certain programs in the school that tend to be invisible, unless you deliberately put them on your radar—important services, delivered by specialists to a handful of students. Zero in on special education classes and designated services such as speech, occupational therapy, adaptive physical education, counseling, second-language acquisition, technology support, and transition programs.

At least twice a year, conduct a special education compliance audit during your routine classroom visits. Get copies of the IEPs for a dozen students to use as a base of inquiry. Read the goals and services on each, then observe the students to see if their daily educational experience matches the letter and the spirit of the IEP document. If not, meet with your special education staff to get into compliance.

If your school is spending a significant amount on technology, it's critical that you can describe the impact of technology on student achievement. When you visit classrooms, try to determine if computers are a reward for good students or a learning tool for all. Is the research capacity of the Internet integrated in a wide spectrum of classroom activities? Has the staff moved beyond emailing each other to more sophisticated applications? Don't rely on enthusiasts for feedback. Canvass classrooms yourself and take notes.

Observe Specific Students

Parents want their kids to be well known by the adults at school, so they light up when principals share vignettes or observations about how their kids perform. They feel more confident about your decisions because "you really know their child." So I made a habit of observing students before I met with parents for IEPs, 504s, suspension conferences, parent-teacher appointments, or the student study team meetings. The more personal and detailed my comments, the more parents were willing to listen, even if I had to give them information that was disappointing or hard to accept.

Observe Short-Term Conditions

Sometimes you want to take the temperature of the school—before statewide testing, after a campus crisis, on Mondays, before an exciting event such as

Halloween or Homecoming. You may need to assess the impact of construction on one section of the school. Are students routed around hazards? Are tools, materials, and machines fenced off? Are workmen clearly identified by name tags or uniforms? Is the noise level acceptable for critical classes? Being proactive about temporary conditions makes staff feel like you're taking care of business. Don't wait for them to call and complain about the jackhammer outside the music room. Tell them what you're doing to mitigate the problem. That sends a message that teaching is your priority, too.

Observe by Time of Day

It's probably a safe bet that early morning at your school looks like a cross between a rodeo and the trading floor of the New York Stock Exchange: dozens of competitive events and everyone baying for attention. Some days you are literally saved by the bell. How does the day begin for your students? If you station yourself in the hallways, you'll discover that some classes start with the precision of a Swiss watch, while in other classes students routinely loiter outside for five minutes, waiting for staff to arrive. In some classes, attendance is taken on the last note of the bell—a thirty-second delay can earn a tardy mark, while other teachers don't take roll at all.

There are other times throughout the day that have a critical impact on student success. Use the following questions to investigate ways to improve the climate for learning.

- What happens during passing periods?
- Is supervision at recess, breaks, and lunch sufficient?
- Are students on free- and reduced-lunch tickets singled out—even unintentionally—in a way that embarrasses them?
- Are nonathletes routinely bullied in the locker room?
- Are special education students segregated at lunch?
- Do students who are bused in mix with students who are not?
- Are there safe havens for students who are socially challenged?
- Are certain areas unofficially reserved for high-status students?
- Are students safe at dismissal, in the parking lot, or at the bus stop?

Having your own learning goal makes each outing a little research project. You don't just loiter around campus. You make a mini-study that gives you more data to use when forming project teams, changing teaching assignments, planning staff development, making budget decisions, and talking to the community.

Digging In: Investigating Teaching and Learning

When you visit classrooms, it's easy to spot who's learning, or at least playing school well. The kids who are talkative, probing, funny, or smart capture your attention and hold it. After ten minutes with a lively group, you can walk out thinking that all's well on the education front. But is it? As educational leaders, we're constantly chanting, *All kids can learn.* But do we mean all kids *will* learn? If that's your goal, you need to ask one essential question every time you enter a classroom: How do all kids learn with this teacher? This line of inquiry embraces a wide variety of teaching strategies, but insists on a nonnegotiable outcome—that individual learning needs must be effectively addressed. Is it clear from the teacher's words and actions that the educational birthright is accessible to all students?

To ensure that, you must train yourself to look systematically at room environments, student-teacher interaction, teaching for understanding—and don't forget those kids on the fringe. What are they learning while the hotshots are waving their hands and vying for attention? The six checklists that follow will help you focus on specific elements and activities that promote student achievement. Photocopy lots of them and keep them handy for your travels around the school.

Classroom Observation Checklists

Characteristics of a Learning Environment. Look for conditions that support learning, including:

_____ Samples of exemplary work with specific feedback on display

_____ Criteria charts, rubrics, or expectations readily visible in the classroom

_____ Evidence of students making choices about what they write, read, investigate, and present

_____ Furniture arrangements that allow individual, small-group, and whole-class work

_____ Written expectations for behavior displayed

_____ Written expectations for subject matter displayed

_____ A variety of learning materials and activities to address different ways of knowing

_____ Discussions that involve many students and points of view

The Teacher as Instructional Expert. Look for evidence that the teacher understands learning.

_____ Content and standards being explicitly taught

_____ A variety of instructional strategies integrated into all lessons

_____ Individual progress monitored

_____ Interventions used for students not demonstrating mastery

_____ A variety of assessment techniques used

_____ Staff development needed to increase effectiveness

_____ Evidence of impact of staff development

Teacher Influence on Learning. Look for patterns of teacher behavior, including:

_____ Gender and racial equity in teacher attention and student participation

_____ Recognition and positive reinforcement of effort as well as work that meets standards

_____ Access to learning for all types of learners

_____ Proportion of teacher talk versus student talk

_____ Students treated as individuals

Characteristics of Knowledge-Building Tasks. Look for evidence that students are expected to:

_____ Grapple with complex ideas and tasks

_____ Communicate ideas clearly, orally and in writing

_____ Plan and organize their own work

_____ Use a variety of resources

_____ Solve authentic mathematical and scientific problems

_____ Create new products and ideas

_____ Transfer prior knowledge to solve problems

_____ Collaborate with peers and adults on projects, drafts, and investigations

Questions to Assess Student Learning. Look at work-in-progress and ask students,

_____ What are you doing?

_____ What are you learning?

_____ Why do you need to know this information?

_____ How is this like other things you've learned?

_____ What will this help you do in the future?

_____ Who helps you understand what you are learning?

_____ What do you do if you get stuck?

_____ How do you know if your work is good enough?

_____ If you want to make your work better, how do you know how to improve it?

_____ Do you talk about your work with your parents or other adults?

Observing Individual Students. Identify one student who is not engaged and watch the student for three to five minutes.

_____ What is the student doing while others are learning?

_____ Where is the student sitting?

_____ How often does the teacher make contact with this student?

_____ How often does the student make contact with the teacher?

_____ What is the nature of the interactions?

Move closer to the student and ask to see some work samples. Then ask,

_____ What do you think this lesson is about?

_____ What would help you understand this better?

_____ What would make it more interesting?

_____ What do you do if you don't understand?

_____ How do you get help?

_____ What's your favorite part of school?

There are lots of ways to document what you are seeing—not for the purpose of formal evaluation, as per the contract, but to provide authentic, data-based feedback for your conversations with teachers, and to help you make decisions about what the staff needs to continue to grow. Here are some ways to capture your observations for later use:

- Use these checklists and write details on the back of each list.
- Keep a notebook with a section for each subject or teacher.
- Carry a clipboard with three-hole punched paper that you can deposit in the notebook when you return to your office.
- Use index cards or Post-it Notes to capture key words that will jog your memory later when you download your head into your computer.
- Carry a laptop if it doesn't inhibit interactions and limit mobility.

Choose the easiest system of documenting and do it faithfully. Soon you'll have a trove of fresh, authentic stories to serve up to staff and community.

Promoting Your Vision: Publicizing Your Observations

One of the most powerful uses of all that observing is to give the staff and community snapshots of the school. Think of it as traveler's tales. You spend your days in places that parents and other teachers rarely see. Don't squander a single scene. Report on what you've seen in classrooms at every public meeting, staff meeting, committee meeting, small gathering, coffee or curbside chat. Remember, you have the power to start a conversation with your staff and community about your vision of teaching and learning. If you use real data from your classroom visits, your remarks are rich with pictures, which speak volumes to parents and professionals. Your traveler's tales have the additional effect of advertising that you're on the job to ensure learning for all kids. Most important, you teach parents how to accurately assess their child's educational experience. When you discuss student work samples, diagram standards, or dissect curriculum with parents, they can replace vague notions—"I think she's a good teacher"—with specific expectations. That's true empowerment.

Gauging Your Impact: Responding to Staff Reactions

Eventually staff members realize that your classroom visits aren't a novelty or a feel-good exercise but rather your way of doing business. What happens then? Some of my best visits were impromptu affairs. Anne Brown, a spectacular multiage teacher, would get me on the phone, insisting "you just have to see what my kids are doing." Excellent teachers, of whom there are so many, are routinely overlooked, while administrators concentrate on coaching their less-effective peers. They're delighted to see you at their door, thrilled to have you break their isolation, and let their students show off for you. As you circulate, you'll get invitations to special events, so be sure to jot down the dates and plan to attend.

It won't be long before you graduate from visitor to collaborator. Teachers will ask advice about instruction, use you as a resource for lesson ideas, or ask you to observe individual students and give them feedback. It was a great day for me whenever I was invited to join in assessments or teaching. Use every visit as an occasion to praise, encourage, and express your appreciation. After a while, morale soars as soon as you cross the doorstep. That's the sign of true leader.

> *"I cannot teach anybody anything. I can only make them think."*
>
> —Socrates

A Rising Tide Lifts All Boats

With frequent focused attention from you, adequate teachers get better. Even the ones who initially don't see your visits as support and company overhear the buzz in the lounge. They catch the air of change and don't want to be left out. Soon their conversations include references to kids. They inquire about training and conferences, and may even invite you in for a specific lesson. This is a wonderful opportunity to help these teachers grow. When you praise what they are doing, they look at themselves in a new way. When you cite their accomplishments in an Applause bulletin, they gain status among the best of their peers.

The Dead-Cat Bounce

Students often confided to me, "he's really nice when you're in the room," of a teacher who more than earned his reputation as a screamer. I knew it was true and longed to take up residence in the room just to prevent him from making shrill remarks to his wary students. Nervous low-end staffers may check in with you after you've made an impromptu visit—"Was there something you wanted when you came in?" They'll explain what students were doing when you arrived, and why it didn't look like teaching or learning. Take the opportunity to give feedback and tell what you would hope to see the next time. You'll see a slight improvement for a day or week—the dead-cat bounce. They straighten up the room or put up a new bulletin board. The momentarily energized may rearrange the chairs if you emphasize cooperative learning, but they can't re-

> *"The purpose of cooking is not the employment of cooks."*
>
> —Anonymous

arrange their attitudes. Mostly they just hope they're not home the next time you come to call.

If students are being severely shortchanged, put these rooms on your Frequent Visits list. Drop by as often as your can, even if you just stay for five minutes. You have a right to be in that classroom. Kids have a right to learn. The union may cry harassment. My response? Only if you bring a sleeping bag and stove.

Subversive Action

I firmly believe that classroom visits are the most direct route to a glorious garden, but they run straight through the heart of the minefield. The reason is that when you pop into a classroom unannounced, you're violating sacred norms, particularly in schools that embrace the cattle-drive approach to education. Cattle-driving teachers say, "Just give me the herd in September and I'll deliver them safely in June. Everything in between is my business." It's an unspoken agreement that guarantees autonomy through noninterference.

The minute you start logging more time in classrooms than in your office, you've broken the pact. For teachers expecting one more cattle drive, your visits are extremely unsettling, and they react in surprising ways. Initially, there's resentment, as if you're questioning their expertise by coming in to take a peek. They literally batten down the hatches to discourage you. Just ignore that unwelcome mat and pull out your master key. If the lesson comes to a screeching halt, just smile and say, "I don't want to interrupt. Please continue!" Then sit down and stay. On your way out, leave a note about one thing in the lesson or room environment that caught your eye.

Some teachers take a more aggressive approach. They antagonize you at meetings or in the hallway, hoping that if they're unpleasant enough, you'll stay away from their rooms. Smile and show up regularly. Another common tactic is to attack your performance as an administrator. Complaints will pour in about issues that you are neglecting. Remarks like "Who's supervising the custodian? The bathrooms are a mess!" are typical red herrings. Or how discipline has eroded under your leadership. You'll hear that things would be better if teachers could just eject kids from class into the disciplinary clutches of the principal, "but you're never in the office when we need you."

The truly determined will leak their complaints to community members, so you encounter an echo at PTA meetings or parent gatherings. Out of the blue someone will ask, "What happens if a teacher has to send a student to the office?" Be prepared with a brief statement, then segue back to "and I'm sure parents agree that supervising instruction is one of my most important responsibilities in this school. It does take a lot of time, but I feel it's the best way to guarantee the your children are getting excellent instruction every day. Here's an example of what I saw today. . . ." That little piece of verbal handiwork lets you control the conversation and deliver your message about what's important for kids. It's a formula—the ABCs of answering tough questions—that you can learn in Chapter 15.

The Payoff

No matter how teachers react, it's all information. Just tell yourself it's a research project—and keep haunting the classrooms. On days when I was reluctant, tired, or discouraged, I would trick myself into visiting by using the Rule of Five—telling myself I would just do five rooms, or stay for five minutes, or only visit five teachers I loved. Inevitably, I stayed longer than I intended, saw more than I imagined, and returned to my work feeling as if I'd spent an hour in some kind of marvelous and refreshing ionizer—or a garden in full bloom.

9
Pruning in the Minefield
Getting Smarter About Evaluation and Dismissal

- The Victory Garden: Evaluation as a Learning Process
- Transforming Underperformers: Designing Improvement Plans
- The Vacant Lot: Preparing for Dismissals
- Bystanders' Syndrome: Dealing with the Fallout
- Trade-Offs: Alternatives to Dismissal

In my first months as principal, I prowled my campus, anxious to discover what I'd inherited. I observed gym classes, coached new teachers, and visited programs that hadn't seen an administrator in years. Each morning after the bell rang, I'd plunge into classrooms, smiling but unannounced. On one of my first outings, I sailed into a room that was as lively as a tomb. Students labored over rows of math problems small enough to make the youngest eyes squint. The teacher was barricaded behind her desk, a Lands' End catalogue draped across her lap. As I approached, she snatched a small sign from the front of her desk and slid it into a drawer. My eyes were sharp enough to catch her stern warning: *The office is closed.* That's how she enforced her splendid isolation—a cardboard sign and a glare for anyone bold enough to approach for help.

By the third week of school, the letters, phone calls, and threats from angry parents were pouring in. I felt like I was on the receiving end of an Amnesty International campaign. One father, fortified with ninety-proof courage, planted himself in the entry hall and announced he wouldn't leave until I removed his child from Lands' End. Another family transferred their child to a school across town, clearly underwhelmed by my leadership. Each week I spent more time listening to frustrated parents and less time sleeping. I observed, coached, conferenced, and valiantly resisted the urge to go after that teacher with a stick.

Just when I thought I couldn't take it much longer, she arrived in my office and announced that she was going into private practice as an educational therapist. I thought it was my first break in the evaluation game. Actually, it was my first lesson.

She returned the next day with the union representative in tow, and denounced me as unsupportive, critical, and a host of other hyperbolic adjectives that I've come to recognize as standard rhetoric in meetings like this. Then she promptly applied for a stress leave and cleared out, leaving me to hustle up a replacement over a long weekend. I issued a brief statement that she was on an illness leave, which no one believed. The community dubbed me a hero for firing her, and the staff freaked out, believing the same. I had a lot to learn.

Girding Your Loins

Very few people appreciate the agony principals experience when they discover the weakest links on their staff. A real low point is when parents ask point-blank, "Why don't you do something? Everyone knows she's incompetent!" You hear yourself mouthing the party line. "It's a personnel matter. I can't discuss it. Please understand, blah-blah-blah, the contract, blah-blah, it's all confidential." You end up feeling like a four-star bureaucrat. It makes you want to bite something.

I once had a group of frustrated parents who formed a committee to dud-proof the school. They didn't want to design new programs but rather to institutionalize the excellent teaching they'd discovered in selected rooms. If they could just make excellence mandatory, their kids would never again get the short straw in the teacher lottery. I wanted to tell them that if it was that easy, I'd be going home at five every day and sleeping through the night.

Nothing you can say will comfort a parent whose child has become so school-phobic that their morning routine includes vomiting and tantrums. Nor can you restore valuable lessons that have been botched by a teacher unwilling or unable to provide the most rudimentary instruction. After a single year with a weak teacher, elementary students perform significantly below their peers with strong teachers. Two or more years in a row, and they may never catch up. Secondary students who miss the fundamentals in math or writing may struggle to pass mandatory exit exams or perform poorly on SATs. That's why ensuring instructional excellence must be a high priority for every principal.

But sadly, the repercussions from firing one incompetent teacher are more fearsome by a factor of ten than they are from totally neglecting the ed-

> *"Not everything that is faced can be changed, but nothing can be changed until it's faced."*
>
> —James Baldwin

ucation of a hundred deserving students. A recent study by the New York State School Boards Association found that the average teacher termination in the Empire State took 319 days and cost $112,000. If the teacher appealed the decision, the cost was likely to top $300,000. In Illinois, the average contested dismissal takes three years and costs $70,000—more if the teacher appeals. And the monetary costs go beyond administrative and legal expenses. In many states, unsatisfactory teachers continue to get paid during the dismissal process—even if they're doing jail time for supplementing their incomes by selling drugs. Is it any wonder that the percentage of tenured teachers fired nationwide has been described as a proxy for zero?

For my money, the most expensive and underreported aspect of evaluation is the high emotional price administrators pay if they attempt a dismissal, or even put a weak teacher on a long-overdue improvement plan. So if you decide to do some pruning in the minefield, expect a battle. Your motives will be questioned. You may be attacked in the local media, or smeared in the union newsletter, scarcely recognizing yourself as the harassing incompetent who doesn't respect teachers. Your evaluation documents will be examined with a fine-tooth comb. You'll be deposed. You may even get a mini-holiday slouching around your local courthouse for a few anxious days—I did. Colleagues will avoid the topic, or shake their heads in quiet wonder. In the end, you may be prodded into signing a letter of recommendation for the unsatisfactory employee. Much later you'll be scandalized by the size of the "stipend" required to settle the case.

On the face of it, there's very little motivation for tackling the deadwood on your staff. It's agonizing, expensive, and consumes enormous amounts of time and energy. Realistically, there are a hundred obstacles between moral outrage and removing a teacher from the profession. In some districts it's nearly impossible—unless you're in the mood for a brisk stoning. That's why lots of administrators just focus on the teachers who can grow and turn a blind eye to the dormant section of the staff. If you opt for 20/20 vision, here's what you'll be facing.

Bring Me Your Huddled Masses

A quick tour around any large campus will make you proud to be in the teaching profession. In room after room, the passion for learning is so powerful, it draws you in like a magnet. Such was the case in Lisa Bartoli's room, where her third-grade students mastered an understanding of how communities work by creating their own city, complete with laws, merchants, local taxes, and even tourists. A brilliant choreographer-turned-teacher named Charlee Cott helped her students translate complex environmental issues into dazzling musicals—producing a compelling union of science and art. Dozens of small garden plots sprang up around the school, thanks to our gardening angels, and the auditorium was gridlocked with singers, actors, and inventors, all learning by doing.

Unfortunately, it's a safe bet that the very schools vigorously promoting excellence also harbor some spectacularly ineffective teachers, such as the ones who view their students as the only downside of an otherwise perfect job. They reduce student-teacher contact to a trickle of widely spaced monosyllables. By piling on long written exercises, they avoid preparation, conversation, and interaction—in a word—teaching. They fill the day with assignments-as-crowd-control, then pore over their gradebooks—looking more like accountants than teachers.

There are also the no-controllers, whose behavior management techniques would be a hit at a circus, but utterly fail to capture youthful attention. Lights flash off and on, like cheap special effects. The plaintive warning, "I'm waiting . . ." only encourages misbehavers to take their time reforming. Some teachers don't manage behavior at all. Impervious to everything, including your arrival, they're busy surfing the Net for home mortgage rates.

Some teachers are so lethargic, you're not sure whether to suggest professional development or apply cardiac paddles. The television is usually on when you arrive. If you sit down to observe, they blink at you, as if emerging from a trance. Refuse to budge, and you may get a whispered explanation of how a blatantly commercial film is directly related to their curriculum.

On the opposite end of the spectrum are teachers who instruct to punish. Some high school instructors boast, "I've never given an A in my whole career—and I never will." They've raised the academic bar so high that they have to stand on tiptoe to keep it beyond all but a handful of gifted students. Daily humiliations goad the rest to try harder, but never produce better students. I find these teachers the most challenging to coach. Convinced that they are exceptional, they see me as the enemy of rigor. But I measure effectiveness with a simple yardstick. Teaching hasn't happened until kids learn. A consistent absence of A's in a class, or a sea of red marks on a set of essays, point to failure, alright! But not on the part of kids. It's a failure to teach well.

The saddest category of underperformers are the good teachers who have simply run out of steam before their retirement kicks in. They've lost the vision, but still need the income, so they benignly preside over classrooms that are oddly lifeless, as if all the natural luminescence has been drained from them.

Most of the underperformers on your staff aren't bad teachers or bad people. They're simply ineffective. They might be teachers who were poorly trained to begin with, and never got additional help. Or they're untrained. Many urban districts are limping along on a willing but largely undercredentialed workforce. The good news is that underperformers can get better—much better—with your support, strategic training, and mentoring. You'll need some skill-and-will on their part. Without that, it's a doomed proposition. But your attitude and actions make the critical difference between ending the year with a victory garden or a vacant lot.

The Victory Garden: Evaluation as a Learning Process

The evaluation process is a huge responsibility, but it can also be a cause for celebration when presented as a way for everyone to learn and grow. The ultimate success of the process is largely determined by the foundation you lay at the beginning of the year. Take time to prepare your whole staff for a successful evaluation experience. Being clear about contractual procedures and your expectations puts you in the best possible position to acknowledge growth, promote improvement, and successfully document a persistently unsatisfactory performance.

- Publish and discuss clear criteria for teacher performance. This may be the toughest part of the whole process, since many contracts feature robust descriptions of who gets first dibs on the parking lot but skip right over criteria for evaluation. In some districts, rigorous professional standards are enforced, while in others, teachers are considered a big success if they take roll accurately and never send kids to the office.
- Publish and discuss the process for determining whether a teacher has adequately satisfied the criteria.
- Discuss each teacher's performance using the published criteria as a framework.
- Establish objectives for improvement.
- Monitor teaching carefully against the objectives using observations, regularly scheduled evaluation conferences, and continuing feedback.
- Document, document, and document.

Transforming Underperformers: Designing Improvement Plans

When you tackle improvement plans with underperforming teachers, you need a mental stance that is constructive and instructive. It always helped me to think of teachers I evaluated as my students. My efforts to help them improve also provided the crucial "support and intervention" evidence that I needed if I decided nonreelection was necessary. The key elements to a successful improvement strategy are:

- Establish a dialogue
- Examine data
- Offer appropriate assistance
- Provide feedback and documentation

Establish a Dialogue

Underperforming teachers are some of the loneliest members of your staff. They're never at the center of exciting collegial discussions. Avoided by supervisiors and marginalized by peers, they may as well be teaching on Mars. So the first thing you need to do is establish contact.

- Praise anything that is praiseworthy. Start with bulletin boards, organization, behavior plans, book displays, content of lectures, enthusiasm for their students, expertise in their subject.
- Ask open-ended questions. Open-ended questions signal that you're not hunting for a single right answer, but want to hear the teacher's thoughts. To answer, teachers have to grapple with ideas about their practices. It's personal. It's challenging. And it can stimulate growth. Your inquiries can trigger a chain reaction that may change a specific lesson or an entire mind-set. Start with these:

    Tell me more about . . .

    What do you think about . . . ?

    What do you do when students don't understand the first time?

    Tell me more about _____ (specific student).

    What has worked in the past?

    What have you done differently in the past?

    How did you decide to use that text?

    How do you decide when to reteach and when to move on?

What comes next?

What are some ways that you check for understanding?

What do you like best about your subject/students?

What would you like to learn more about?

What would you do differently if you could change one thing?

Open-ended questions raise the anxiety level of teachers—and that's good. Many of them have not actually thought about why they do certain things for a long time. These inquiries also keep you in a listening mode, which is critical for effective intervention and growth. Very few people change just because someone talks to them. If that worked, all those mandated training sessions would have produced miracles on the order of Lourdes.

Examine Data

Underperforming teachers need concrete examples of their performance targets. You need evidence that their students are learning. Examining data together is the most effective way to provide both. Look at a variety of student work samples together: group projects, homework, drafts, and assessments. Borrow work from similar classes to provide models for standards-based lessons and rubrics. Look at test scores to identify which students aren't succeeding and discuss why. Ask more questions, such as

Tell me about this assignment.

What skills were you trying to emphasize or assess?

How did they learn how to do this?

What were other ways they worked at mastering this skill?

Tell me about the rubric/criteria you use for judging the success of the work?

How did you share the rubric/criteria with students before they did the assignment?

How will students who were not successful on this effort work to master this skill?

Don't try to rebuild an underperforming teacher from the ground up. Agree on two or three improvement goals based on your dialogue and review of student data. Be clear that you expect concentration and progress on these specific goals. Document your agreement and try to cast a blind eye on any other deficiencies.

Offer Appropriate Assistance

A growing number of states and districts have created peer assistance and review systems to address professional improvement from within the teaching ranks. The teachers themselves agree to review the performance of veterans and novices. This program shifts the role of the union from protecting weak teachers to establishing, enforcing, and mentoring for higher standards of teacher quality. Experienced teachers coteach, observe, model, prescribe interventions, and recommend disciplinary measures, including dismissal. Under peer review, the number of teachers recommended for dismissal has increased.

If you don't have a formal peer review program, suggest coteaching sessions or arrange for struggling teachers to observe their peers, then conference afterward about what they saw and how they can use that information in their own lessons. Find mentors on your staff, at other sites, at the central office, or at the university. Teachers who want to improve may not feel free to admit their shortcomings to the person who also writes the final report. Recruiting a peer or mentor gives the teacher a safer source of support, and gives you the distance you need to objectively assess progress.

Poorly trained teachers need to observe excellent models. Send in a sub to free them up, or take over their class for an hour to give youself a treat. Send them with a strong team to professional development sessions, then have a guided discussion afterward about what they learned and how they intend to use their new knowledge to improve instruction. Observe for follow-through in the classroom.

Working to improve staff is an excellent use of your time. But if you single-handedly play mentor to a failing teacher, you run the risk of being labeled as a failure yourself. *You worked with this person, she did everything you asked, and you still want to fire her? You're the one who failed!*

Provide Feedback and Documentation

Employees need specific, descriptive feedback to document their progress toward improvement goals, and to encourage them to keep trying. They'll appreciate hearing that their efforts are paying off.

- Use descriptive language such as:

    You planned activities to stimulate students with more advanced skills and to engage those mastering the basics.

    You displayed samples of student work to provide clear expectations.

You developed complete lesson plans for a week of biology investigations.

You reduced the noise level in your classroom through a positive behavior plan, so instruction is more coherent.

You observed 504 plans by making modifications for students when necessary.

- Visit often and look for signs of improvement. Document every visit and intervention. You may want to get a small spiral notebook for each person you're observing. Palm pilots are also excellent.
- Share your observations in writing with the teacher. Be sure to sign and date your notes and keep a copy in a file for yourself.
- Conference regularly and refer to your notes during the conference.
- Discuss alternative job assignments. What are some other areas of expertise? What else would they like to try? What have they done happily or successfully in the past? You never can tell when a better match will come along and you will both be prepared to make the move.

Many times, a combination of these interventions can boost a marginal teacher into the adequate range, and that's a huge step for which you can both feel proud. I've seen zealots rise from the ashes of a stalled career through strong professional development and support. Helping a veteran rediscover the joy of teaching is a real honor. If none of this works, you may be heading down that long and lonesome road that leads to nonreelection.

The Vacant Lot: Preparing for Dismissals

It's your professional obligation to make every effort to help staff improve, and it's a moral obligation to the students in their classes. To visualize the impact of your efforts, multiply every improvement by the thirty, sixty, one hundred, or more students with whom that improved teacher has contact each day.

However, occasionally you'll encounter a teacher who is impervious to interventions. In that case, you have a legal duty to notify and document unsatisfactory performance. That doesn't necessarily mean firing, but at the very least, you're going to be pen pals. Before you move toward dismissal, ask yourself these questions:

Is there a different assignment this employee could do effectively?

Could this employee improve with some accommodations or modifications?

Could this employee improve with different supervision?

Have I sufficiently documented the employee's failure to perform?

Have I documented suggestions and directions for improvement?

Will the district support me during the dismissal process?

Don't assume—ask. Then, if all answers point toward the exit, line up your advisors, memorize the time lines, and remember—there's no such thing as a no-brainer when you're going for dismissal. You'd think a teacher who sells drugs would be history. Not so. How about the one who decks a kid? Still teaching. Tanqueray in a glue bottle? Working steadily—more or less. You can lose. You can make a deal. An outright victory is nearly impossible. But if the incompetent's name disappears from your roster, you'll feel like a winner.

Polish the Armor

The minute you start to thin the deadwood on your staff, the union will be notified. Sometimes this can work to your advantage. The first year I was principal, our district had a wonderful union leader who encouraged failing teachers to rethink their career plans, and commiserated with me when it didn't work. She could be tough, but I always felt that she was fair.

The climate between teachers' unions and administrators varies wildly from one district to the next. You could be chatting over coffee with your union president, while another principal has a permanent place on the hot seat. But the big picture has improved significantly since national union leaders embraced the idea that their role goes beyond protecting teachers from management and negotiating universal benefits. Union leaders increasingly promote the idea that teachers should organize to raise student achievement by providing effective training, enforcing quality standards, and, in some states, weeding out unsatisfactory colleagues. Twenty-four districts, the largest being New York City's AFT, are participating in the Teacher Union Reform Network project (TURN). TURN's misson is to take the lead in building and sustaining high-performing schools for all students. They are determined to seek higher levels of student achievement and improve the quality of the teaching force.

Whether your working relationship with the union is harmonious or harrowing, you need to be prepared for lots of questions if you're considering a dismissal, such as: How have you provided support for this teacher if you thought she wasn't doing a good job? How many days did you go in her class? What actions did you take there? Did you consult with her afterward? What was the result of those meetings? Did you document your interventions? Reach for your documentation file to provide evidence of multiple interventions and good-faith efforts. Without a paper trail, it's your word against theirs and that won't be enough for a hearing officer. It won't impress your supervisor, either.

Have lots of chairs in your office, because teachers under fire may arrive with a squadron of union representatives, observers, and note takers, just to rattle you. Younger teachers may shun the union staff and bring their own lawyers.

It's still no fun.

If the meeting is very adversarial, the union staff may pepper you with contract language, often their own interpretations. While you're trying to focus on the conference, they'll raise procedural challenges. If a contract question is raised, acknowledge it, and say that you will research it later. Then refocus on the teacher's performance. It takes a will of iron to maintain your composure in these meetings, but you can do it if you keep asking yourself, "What's best for kids?"

> *"In matters of principle, stand like a rock."*
> —Thomas Jefferson

Don't do these meetings alone. Have your own note taker, preferably a coadministrator or district representative. Debriefing afterward with your scribe will help you strategize and sharpen your case. And the day may come when you need a witness. Be prepared.

The Paper Trail

If you are seriously considering a dismissal, you should consult regularly with personnel, the human resources director, or an assistant superintendent in charge of personnel. Another great resource is *A Survival Guide to Teacher Layoffs* by Lillian Lee Port (1997). If you have a good working relationship with the union president, let her know where you are heading and why.

But your main focus must be on documenting your efforts to help the failing teacher improve. If you conference with him fifty-seven times, model impeccable lessons, provide instructional interventions that could earn you a doctorate from Columbia Teachers' College, and pay for a live-in mentor out of your own pocket but fail to document, you may as well stay in your office and watch Oprah on a portable television.

The toughest part of documentation is disciplining yourself to make this letter-writing campaign a priority in the midst of more urgent or satisfying work. Remind yourself that if a dismissal is challenged—and most are—the case will be built on your letters to the unsatisfactory employee. So you need to create a structured correspondence. It sounds burdensome, but like many things bureaucratic, there's a formula. Follow it, and your lawyers can do the rest.

Legally sufficient disciplinary letters contain five critical elements. They are:

1. A clear description of what the employee did that is unsatisfactory.
2. A statement of what the employee should have done.
3. The effect of the unsatisfactory behavior or performance.
4. What you expect the employee to do in the future, how you will help, and the consequences if there is no improvement.
5. The right of the employee to respond, including time lines and whether your letter will be placed in the permanent file.

A condensed version of such a letter might look something like this.

> Dear Mr. Driscoll,
>
> On September 26, 2001, your left your third-period gym class unsupervised while you talked on your cell phone in the weight room. Your conduct violated the Athletic Employee's Handbook and the Education Code, both of which state that students engaged in athletics must be supervised at all times by a credentialled person.
>
> During your absence, three students who were skirmishing on the field got into an argument, which escalated to a fistfight. All three students were suspended under our zero-tolerance policy, resulting in a disruption to their studies. One student lost a front tooth. The district has received a claim from the parents for the emergency dental work.
>
> Henceforth, you are to remain with your students at all times. Failure to comply with this directive will result in a formal letter of reprimand. If you need to make an emergency phone call, please contact the administrative staff and someone will cover your class while you use the phone.
>
> A copy of this letter will be placed in your personnel file after ten days. You may prepare a response and have it attached to this document.

One letter, written late in the year, will not make your case. Start drafting letters like this the minute you sense that things aren't going well. Keep working on all the positive interventions, document your support plan, and above all, memorialize every major infraction with a disciplinary letter.

Bystanders' Syndrome: Dealing with the Fallout

If you actually succeed in dismissing a teacher, or helping some staffers make another career choice, relief is immediately replaced by the challenge of dealing with the Bystanders' Syndrome. Suddenly there's a hole in the staff roster and a new face at the staff meeting, without the usual going-away bagels. You cannot talk openly about the Disappeared One without risking a breach of confidentiality, but the ex-employee can, and will. The telephone tree becomes a forest of gossip. Parents loyal to the teacher may rally and even picket the school. You're portrayed as the professional brute—robbing a defenseless teacher of his livelihood and mental health. You'll be sorely tempted to counter with "What about the kids' right to expert instruction?" Think it, to keep yourself strong, but don't say it. Open your mouth and you'll be eating your words at a hearing. Teachers pay hefty union dues. They expect representation—and get it.

Firings and resignations are seismic events in any school. The reaction of the rest of the staff is brief but palpable. In a single act, you've been redefined. To some staffers, you've gone from mild-mannered administrator to Lizzie Borden. Others are impressed that someone finally had the guts to call a spade a spade. Your devotees may admire your courage, but worry about your shelf life. Marginal teachers will probably feel insecure or threatened. And the true believers of organized labor will cloak themselves in outrage, then attack. All of them are reacting to the exercise of power.

What you need to convey to your staff is that you will exercise appropriate power to ensure that children are safe and receiving the instruction they deserve. Redouble your praise and recognition for teachers who are making daily efforts toward your common goals. Increase the number of "Bravos" in your weekly bulletin. Reinforce standards through recognition. Good teachers get the message that they are safe and appreciated. The rest are on notice.

Trade-Offs: Alternatives to Dismissal

Many administrators have been so gouged by the process of firing one unsatisfactory teacher that they vow "never again." Some are so offended by the specter of unions defending professional malpractice that they abandon the profession entirely. But many administrators have found ways to improve their staffs without resorting to dismissals. Here are some of the other choices:

- Keep the pressure on underperforming staff members through observations and conferences and hope they will resign or transfer. Some teachers submit a letter of resignation when dismissal is near, and then you can work together to put the best face on their departure.
- Create new assignments that use the talents of staff who are no longer effective in the classroom, or build strong teams around them.

- Trade a satisfactory letter of recommendation for a voluntary transfer, and feel marginally better for it. You're passing the lemon, but you must be an advocate for your own school, first and foremost.

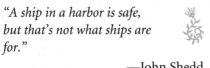

> *"A ship in a harbor is safe, but that's not what ships are for."*
>
> —John Shedd

- Some principals simply ignore the deadwood and focus on the segment of the staff that can grow. That strategy has its price, usually in the hours you spend talking to unhappy parents.

The Price of Pruning

Evaluation and dismissal are, without a doubt, the most corrosive parts of the job. Incompetent teachers consume hours and hours of administrator time, while robbing kids of their education—often the ones who need it the most. If you inherit a school where evaluations have always been end-of-the-year-sign-on-the-line formalities, or didn't happen at all, you have a rough road ahead. If you're a conscientious evaluator, you will be exhausted and anxious lots of the time. On the other hand, you'll be exhausted and disgusted if you don't at least try. But only you can decide what you can survive, what you can abide, and what's the best use of your time.

10

The In-Box Never Sleeps

Getting Smarter About Communication Systems

- Restrict
- Redirect
- Regulate

It's hard to imagine any principal satisfying the communication appetites of people who complain about the ten seconds it takes to connect to the Internet, and hence to the entire planet. "You didn't get my message?" they cry in disbelief. "I left it an hour ago!" An hour is like a decade for a busy principal, filled with hundreds of interactions, mostly of the semiurgent persuasion.

As a school administrator, you work in a complex, information-glutted world. While your 1950s counterpart dealt with phones, postal deliveries, and a handful of deferential humans, you are pelted with a hail of communications, including faxes; email; voice mail; school, district, and express mail; cell-phone messages; instant messages; beepers; walkie-talkies; subpoenas; Post-its; handwritten notes; phones; and more human interactions than a lone cashier at the after-Christmas sales.

It's no wonder you end up feeling like an information ATM. Twelve to fifteen hours a day, you're open for business, and business is always good. Or is it? Talking to people is a huge part of your job, but being reduced to a human ATM is not. It's inefficient and exhausting. Some days you talk until your jaws ache, but no one seems to hear. Or they hear something you never said, so you have to start all over again. Answering questions could become your full-time job, but you already have one—*asking essential questions*. You need to spend your days deep in conversation with teachers about curriculum, instructional excellence, and achievement for all students.

The challenge then, is to safeguard time for this vital work while keeping ahead of the communication demands pouring into your school through every mail slot and modem. Since there's only one of you and a legion of information seekers in hot pursuit, you could end up as roadkill on the information highway, unless you master three strategies for managing communication systems.

Restrict

While most of the world seems intent on connecting to every sensate being and cable channel between here and Mars, I'm recommending that you launch a quiet campaign to restrict the communication systems in your office. Silence the voice mail, have an unlisted email address, and say no to casual visits that consume precious time earmarked for classroom visits. Sounds crazy? Maybe, but it's a brand of insanity that puts student achievement first. That still seems right—even in the twenty-first century. But don't take my word for it. Pay attention to the amount of time consumed by the phone, email, and interruptions in your average day, and then see if you think your students are getting their fair share of you.

If you explain your communication policy in that context, the community may rethink their demands on your time. They may be less than thrilled about getting a return call from your secretary instead of bending your ear for half an hour, but few will say that your time is misspent.

Voice Jail

Some days I imagine the inventor of voice mail sitting in a quiet cubicle, thinking up new ways to torment me; thinking long chains of uninterrupted thoughts because he doesn't have a phone. Meanwhile, for every parent phone call I earnestly return, fourteen new messages arrive. I'm in voice jail and it's a no-win situation. Beside the unrelenting volume, people make assumptions about voice mail that are preposterous but, nonetheless, will get you in trouble. They include:

- If they leave a message, you get it immediately.
- You will call back, if only to say that you got the message.
- Their message will be a priority, even over children or staff.

There are other problems with having your very own voice mail. It gives the community twenty-four-hour access to you, which means that during the scant six or seven hours when you manage to find your way home, your phone is manning a drive-through window. It's more than discouraging to stay late, dutifully returning calls, then arrive back at the crack of dawn to find the red message-light blinking a silent nag. Not responding quickly will get you a bad reputation in service-minded communities—and there is no such thing as quickly enough.

Voice-mail messages are inefficient. Many people ramble for whole minutes, pausing, um-ing and uh-ing, then hurriedly mumble their phone number so you have to replay the message three times just to catch the last two numerals. Big waste.

The most detrimental aspect of voice mail for me was the emotional impact of listening to complaining or abusive people, especially at the end of a grueling day. If your guard is down, you end up with a gut full of resentment. It's bad for your health. So unless your boss insists on voice mail for all administrators, pull the plug. Use your phone for outgoing calls and have your staff record your messages on NCR pads. Paper messages are superior to voice mail because you can

- Peruse them quickly and prioritize. With voice mail, the most important call may be number thirty-one, and you won't even get to seventeen without an interruption.
- Jot a response on the message and have staff return the call.
- Carry messages with you until you reach a phone or have a break.
- Throw them away if you've already dealt with the situation.
- Clip them to pages of your daybook for later reference/reminder.
- Get the facts without the affect.

An alternative is to keep your voice mail but have a member of your support staff download it twice a day, recording all information onto a phone log that includes columns for the name of the caller, phone number, the message, and your reply. Review the log at intervals throughout the day, jot down replies, and have staff return as many calls as possible. Give them a simple script. "I am calling for _____, the principal. She received your message and asked me to tell you . . ." Staff can check off or highlight returned calls to create a record. You only return the calls that need your personal touch.

Do the Math: The Perils of Email

As principal, I had a love-hate relationship with email. I loved keeping in touch with educators and authors around the country, loved sending messages to colleagues across town on a Saturday morning and discovering that they, too, were slouching in jeans at their desks, catching up. But I hated the volume—from twenty to forty messages per hour, largely generated by a staff of only fifty.

Do the math. One message per staff person, five days a week, plus district and professional messages could easily net you four hundred transmissions by sundown on Friday. If you take a mere minute to read, answer, or delete each message, you have almost seven hours online just to catch up. Distribute your email address to parents and you can type until your carpal tunnels cry "Uncle!" but you'll never be more than a dead-letter office.

The other unfortunate reality of email is the potential for personal messages to be forwarded, edited—in effect, "published" without your knowledge. You must consider exposure when you communicate electronically. If parents have serious concerns that they want to share with you, encourage them to put the details in a letter to you, then call or conference with them.

A final word on the instant-messaging world. Clearly, I am at the Victorian end of the spectrum. At the other end are the principals who adore email—so much that they refuse to accept paper messages from their staff. It's a personal preference, but I strongly suggest that you do the math. Believe me, the world will still beat a path to your door, even if you unplug the phone, trash your monitor, and plunge your office into pitch darkness.

Interruptions

Speaking of a path to your door, interruptions are the third great time-consumer in a principal's day. They're unscheduled, unexpected, and always take longer than you think. "Do you have a minute?" never means sixty seconds. It can be an hour of psychodrama that exhausts you. Or three rounds of regulation boxing, and you without your gloves. Or a litany so long you think you've stumbled into the Vatican. But it's never sixty seconds.

However, interruptions are part of the job, and frequently give you a chance to advance your agenda. So don't bar the door. The point of managing communication is not to minimize contact with people, especially staff, but to maximize the time you spend talking about the essential work of the school. To keep your focus, learn to reduce or reframe the three most common interruptions in a principal's day—from parents, staff, and yourself.

Parent Interruptions. Parents are ingenious about snaring a few minutes of face-time with you. Some queue up outside your office at the crack of dawn, as if you're giving away Superbowl tickets. Others take a shortcut past your office on their way to the PTA mailbox, or shadow you like a secret service agent as you walk around campus. I had a parent climb through the shrubbery outside my window on a Sunday afternoon, trying to enroll her child.

Parents like this usually just want the best for their kids. The problem is, they want it now. You need to use diplomacy and caution to establish access with boundaries. You cannot provide unrestricted availability to parents—that belongs to staff and students—so consider reserving a portion of each week for parent conferences. Publish your schedule in every parent bulletin, post it on bulletin boards, and give it to your support staff. Then you can be friendly and firm with gate-crashers. Greet them cordially, then guide them to your calendar to schedule an appointment. Mention that you can't talk for long, as you are due in classrooms, but assure them that you are looking forward to talking later in the week.

Always clarify the topic of the appointment, but avoid details unless you want to have the whole conference twice. There are two reasons to identify the topic in advance. The most important reason is to safeguard your relationship with your teachers. Parents often come directly to you about classroom problems, cutting the teacher out of the loop. Professional protocol and many contracts require that teachers get the first stab at problem solving. If parents haven't spoken directly to the teacher, they must. Don't budge on this. Ninety-five percent of the time, that's the last you'll hear from them. If they're still unsatisfied after meeting with the teacher, you will need to get involved.

The other reason to identify the topic is so that—like a good Boy Scout—you can be prepared. If a parent wants to discuss the board policy on dual enrollment, and you don't have a clue, there's time to get smarter. Have one of your staff call the board secretary to get a copy of the text and any relevant points of controversy. The Internet can also provide data for parent meetings. Twenty minutes of research will help you hold up your end of a productive conversation.

If a parent claims, "It's an emergency!" you still might not be able to have a full meeting. Take five minutes, get the Readers' Digest version of the story, and schedule an appointment or phone conference for later that day. Remember, if your door is open to anyone seeking an impromptu chat, they'll go home content, but you'll burn the midnight oil.

Staff Interruptions. Staff interruptions are opportunities to promote your vision and improve morale. Consider this scenario: a teacher thrusts her head in your door, apologizes for interrupting, and you reply, "It's no problem. I was hoping I'd see you today. That lesson you did yesterday on local elections was outstanding. Now how can I help you?" In just three seconds you managed to praise, reinforce best practices, and convey your eagerness to help. Interruptions are opportunities.

Teachers interrupt because they're on the fly with only minutes between classes and fierce competition for your attention. Try to be available for them, especially before school and during their breaks, and whenever appropriate, respond to their needs immediately. If you can't stop and talk, here are two ways to avoid frustration all around. Ask them to be very concise about their request and then get back to them by phone or message as soon as possible. Or say, "I could drop by your room at 2:00. Would that work?" Write it in your daybook or palm pilot and show up.

Have a door policy to facilitate communications with staff. An open door means you're available; if it's closed, only interrupt for emergencies. Put a pen and Post-it Notes outside when you must close your door, and encourage people to stick notes on the door. When you emerge, jot an answer on the Post-it Notes, and have your support staff get back to them quickly. And use every junket around the campus as an opportunity to give quick and timely answers, reducing frustration for staff and interruptions when you finally get back to your office.

Self-Interruptions. Controlling interruptions begins at home. There are a hundred ways you can distract yourself from the work at hand, especially if it's unpleasant or beyond the realm of your energy and skills. You sit down to write a budget report, but leap up as if the chair were spring-loaded, seized by the need for caffeine. Lurching toward the coffeepot, you realize that a cookie would really hit the spot, so you wander over to the cafeteria, or stare longingly into the vending machines, hoping for a gastronomic miracle. Then you pore over a thesaurus, searching for clever ways to say "not enough money to do the job right," call the fiscal office for help, and get voice mail. But since your Rolodex is open—why not ring an old friend you haven't talked to in months? Anything to avoid the inevitable.

Sometimes you interrupt yourself because you're just too exhausted or stressed to push one more inch. Don't treat yourself like a galley slave. Take a break. Chapter 14 "Living Well Is the Best Revenge," is full of ideas to revive your energy and outlook in just a few minutes. Be kind to yourself—your attitude and the quality of your work will improve.

An untidy desk or office might be the biggest distracter of all. Every attempt to get down to work results in a mad scramble for files or faxes that have gone missing in the avalanche where your in-box was last reportedly seen. These impromptu search parties consume hours of valuable time in fruitless sorting and fuming, sapping the little energy you'd reserved for the task itself. So tidy up and read on for systems to control incoming paperwork. It could reduce interruptions significantly.

Another possibility? The furniture. A set of comfortable chairs beckons to visitors, unless there's a pile of books on each seat. If your desk faces the door, everyone who walks by feels compelled to make eye contact or say, "hi." I angled my desk toward the windows, and drank in the sight of trees and rain on days when I never left the building. Finally, if there are items in your office that other people need every day, move them out or buy duplicates to reduce traffic. And fix that broken desk drawer instead of yanking on it ten times a day. There are better ways to get your exercise!

Redirect

As a new principal, I wasn't a quick study in delegating. It seemed very top-downish, with a taint of dumping. After years in the classroom, doing everything for myself, you could say I was delegationally challenged. If a task landed on my desk, I assumed it was mine. If I observed a logistical problem with the cafeteria or traffic snarls at dismissal, I was on the case. I typed my own correspondence, took and returned phone calls, calligraphied welcome signs for the first day of school, and replaced broken sprinkler heads. In my zeal to do everything well, I overlooked two glaring facts: (1) There was a lot more of everything than there was of me, even if I took up residence in my office, and (2) I wasn't always the best person for the job.

I had a lot to learn.

Life improved as soon as I replaced *delegate* with *redirect*. The idea of redirection is simple. You handle all the tasks that are appropriately yours, but redirect all other tasks to the people who can do them best. To make redirection a success, make sure staff members understand what needs to be done, possess the skills to do it, and have the authority to make decisions to complete the task independently. It's the basis of good management and good customer service, but it's also a powerful tool for empowering staff.

> "Never tell people how to do things. Tell them what to do and they will surprise you with their ingenuity."
>
> —George S. Patton

I was blessed with a smart staff who took to redirection like ducks to water. Our first enrollment season together was a nightmare. Parents swarmed into the school from dawn 'til dusk, thrusting their paperwork across a counter the size of a breadboard. Long lines made them cranky, bureaucratic regulations made them worse; the baying could be heard for blocks. Not a pretty sight—and the office staff bore the brunt of it.

Even as a rookie, I knew there had to be a better way, so once things settled down, I asked the office staff what would work better for them, and let them tinker with the process until they got it perfect. The next year, enrolling families had individual, sit-down appointments in a private room. Ten minutes—in and out. No lines. No baying. We even closed the office for lunch. The solution was simple. Staff understood the problem. I gave them the authority to fix it. The enrollment nightmare vanished.

Redirecting Your Thinking

I trained myself to redirect tasks by asking a few simple questions each time I snatched a memo off my desk or observed a problem that needed attention.

- Is this a good use of my time?
- Whose job is this, anyway?
- Who has this information?
- Who is trained to do this best?
- Who has the best ideas for assessing this problem and working toward a solution?
- Who has a real investment in its success?

Redirecting acknowledges that the people on your support team are the experts in areas where you are not. It sends a message to administrative assistants, cafeteria workers, instructional aides, the librarian, assistant principal, custodian, and teachers that you trust them to make decisions about problems or new tasks, and restructure their work for greater efficiency, because they know best. When you redirect, use phrases that reinforce those expectations, such as:

> at a time that works best with your schedule
>
> as often as you think necessary
>
> as efficiently as possible
>
> as soon as you determine a need
>
> when you anticipate a shortage
>
> or devise a system that works better for you
>
> until you no longer need it
>
> until we retrain staff to your new system

Let staff make as many decisions as possible until they give you reason to doubt, then work with them on decision making. And don't just redirect simple tasks. Encourage innovation and improvements that require new information. If the problem is complex, have staff think about solutions, come up with their best thinking, and meet with you to fine-tune their ideas. Once they know that you expect them to take the initiative, suggestions will multiply.

Supporting Redirection

When staff members take on new responsibilities, provide support. Have someone who is familiar with the task do a side-by-side or a mini-seminar, then be available as a mentor. And it is critical to remember that when you redirect tasks, they don't need to be done exactly as you would have—only as well as necessary. Here are some tasks you should redirect:

- Phone calls requesting concrete information such as dates, time, prices, rules: give them to support staff
- Emails requesting similar information: forward to the appropriate person for response
- Xeroxing, collating, mailing, distributing: give to support staff
- School schedules: those most affected, usually teachers, can organize, revise, and publish
- Requests from staff for board policy or education code information: redirect to central office staff
- Responses to central office surveys: support staff can orchestrate
- Students events: students can make PA announcements
- Assistant principals should do many principals' tasks with support and feedback to gain skill and confidence.
- Administrative staff should systematize their work, creating or revising forms, procedures, and bulletins to streamline their work and respond effectively to staff and community.

Redirecting Teacher Inquiries

Teachers ask a zillion questions, many of which are perfect candidates for redirection. For example, some people are careless about mundane information, like testing dates or when rainy-day lunch ends. They get the announcements along with everyone else, but forget or misunderstand, so they come back again and again. This is not a good use of your time, so give them your friendliest broken-record routine. Refer them to the published source, and eventually they'll pester someone else or read your bulletins.

Frequent, same-subject queries are a critique of your communication skills. If you get ten questions about the inclement weather schedule or the new staff parking plan, you're not being clear. Review and rewrite your bulletins until a disinterested outsider could understand them without help, and check the distribution system for gaps.

Some teacher-questions are thoughtful observations that deserve wider discussion and may hold the seeds of a project. Set up a column in your staff bulletin to broadcast fertile questions to the whole staff. Informal discussions may yield simple solutions or new project teams will sprout to take action.

You've probably sensed that some teachers don't want information as much as contact. Their initial questions are just a way to get close to you. Use their overtures as an opportunity to talk about your common efforts, what you have observed in their rooms, or suggestions for collaboration. Reward their effort to connect with authentic interest and feedback. Eventually, they'll skip the warm-up question and get right to the main event.

Regulate

I was always amazed at the amount of paper that poured into my office on any given day. It made me want to send a donation to the Tree People. Most of it arrived while my back was turned, which meant urgent faxes were cohabiting with junk mail. Without a system, I had to dig through the drifts to discover that an enrollment report was long overdue, and the head of the fiscal department was hunched over his fax like a gargoyle, waiting for my reply.

> *"I love deadlines. I like the whooshing sound as they fly by."*
>
> —Douglas Adams

So I devised a few simple systems with my support staff to regulate the traffic. I set up a series of folders and boxes on the counter next to my desk as my communications headquarters, and I checked it briefly each time I returned to my office.

- Faxes were tucked in a bright green folder, boldly labeled FAX. If they required an immediate reply, I wrote directly on them and passed them back to staff to be returned.
- The twenty-four-hour box held anything that needed my attention before I went home.
- Red folders were labeled for time-line sensitive documents such as staff evaluations, safety reports, and budget worksheets.

- The seat of my chair was the place for burning issues that were just short of the three-bell alarm used to pry me from classrooms. The minute I walked into my office, I checked the chair.

> *"Everything should be made as simple as possible, but not simpler."*
>
> —Albert Einstein

- Many principals sit with their administrative assistants for thirty to forty-five minutes at the end of each day to review communications and orchestrate responses.

Phone Booth with a View

If you've restricted your phone calls as suggested, by the end of the day you'll have a pile of messages or a phone log waiting for you. This is the time to be very disciplined. Set aside a specific time for returning calls, close your door, hang out the Do Not Disturb sign, or go into hiding. Cell phones mean you have a lot more freedom, so be creative. If sitting atop the bleachers watching track events feels relaxing, that's your phone booth. How about the referee's chair on the tennis court or the picnic table under the trees? Your campus may have a half-dozen places-with-a-view that will energize you enough to push through your call-back pile. However, if you're still answering your own voice mail, you'll be tethered to your desk, straining your weary ears to understand those muffled messages.

Now try some techniques to keep your calls efficient. Your chances of getting a machine are at least fifty-fifty, but there are those rare people who call you and then actually wait by the phone.

- If a person answers, say, "This is _____ returning your call. How may I help you?" Get to the point in a customer-friendly manner. Avoid chitchat.
- If you get a machine, leave a brief but clear message, including the time that the person should try to reach you the next day. That satisfies your immediate obligation and puts the ball back in their court.
- If you don't have time to talk, call and say so: "I'm on my way to the board meeting, but I just wanted you to know that I got your message, and I will call you tomorrow before ten. Will that work?"
- If you have a pile of "duty" calls, dial at least one family to say how well their kids are doing and give an example from your classroom visits or a teacher report. You'll get a rush of industrial-strength gratitude that helps ward off phonephobia.

Limited Access, Undivided Attention

Communities can seem voracious in their need for your attention. The better you are at your job, the more they want you. I used to go to my office on weekends to get a jump on Monday, and when the word got out, I found myself conferencing with apologetic but determined parents, who tapped on the front door or waited on the porch for me to emerge. In self-defense, I locked the doors, closed the blinds, and worked like mad. That hermit routine is okay for Sundays, but woe to the administrator who erects weekday barricades.

Let the community know that you're eager to meet with them by appointment, then set up a system of limited access with undivided attention. Some principals set aside one hour twice a week, for twenty-minute appointments. Announce your plan and the person to contact. Always keep your appointments, unless the building is on fire. Be punctual. If the meeting isn't over in twenty minutes, schedule a second meeting for the following day or week.

Now here's the trick. Even though the meeting is short, people can walk away feeling satisfied, if you give them your undivided attention. Get out from behind your desk. Have some comfortable chairs, even if you have to buy them yourself. Sit back and relax. Don't answer the phone. Never do paperwork. Always make eye contact.

Some of these meetings will be fascinating. Parents show up with a glimmer of an idea, and fifteen minutes later, a project is born. Some meetings are less entertaining. Disgruntled parents are the first to fill your dance card. But you can keep your stress level down using some of these self-preservation techniques.

- Limit the duration. Remind parents that you have a schedule, and stick to it. Rationing time frequently results in more efficient meetings.
- Schedule meetings back-to-back so you have to move on.
- Schedule meetings before mandatory events, so you have to stop.
- Tell yourself that no matter how bad it gets, it will only last for twenty minutes.
- Ask yourself, "What can I learn from this?" It helps you be a better observer.
- Ask yourself, "How will I feel when this is over?" It will help you anticipate relief and picture yourself surviving. You may even begin to smile.
- Arrange for a bailout. If you can't set limits overtly, ask your assistant

to call with your "next appointment" or even an "emergency" at an appointed time to spring you from the meeting.

- Repeat the phrase from Nietzsche: Anything that doesn't kill me strengthens me.

Some principals prefer a more informal, group approach. They have drop-in coffees one morning a week. There's no agenda—just coffee and conversation. Whoever shows up gets to ask questions, voice concerns, and seek advice. These coffees can feel riskier than private meetings, because there's always the chance you'll be put on the spot, and fumble in front of an audience. So consider your strengths and the temperament of your community, then establish some form of access on your terms.

The Dangers

The downside to restricting, redirecting, and regulating is that instead of winning accolades as the great communicator, the frustrated or disappointed may label you as distant or afraid. And in some cultures, a twenty-minute meeting is downright impossible, since courtesy demands at least ten minutes of pleasantries before embarking on the subject at hand. Some parents are offended when you insist that they make an appointment because you're due in classrooms all morning—isn't that what teachers are for? People with chronic problems want to cast you in a fix-it role and may feel hurt when you set boundaries. Just keep reminding the community that you are the quality-control devise in the school, and you can't do that job from a chair in your office. Don't let the criticism deter you from your mission.

The Oracle

On the flip side, there are parents and staff who will never drop by, never lob a question in your direction, yet they remain fully informed by making regular visits to the local oracle—your office manager. School surveys confirm that many people view the office staff as their primary source of information, which explains why your support staff has such a tough time keeping ahead of their work. It also underscores the importance of meeting with your office staff regularly. Share facts, dates, and the latest issue that may create a stir. If there's talk of a change in the permit policy or the length of the school day, they will be bombarded with panic calls. Ask what they're hearing and clarify what you know to be fact. Work with them to develop scripts for tough questions, so you can to control the message.

This is especially important during turbulent times when rumormongers drop by, prospecting for provocative sound bites. Taken out of context, their whispers can break the land-speed record between your office and the parking lot. Some are simply gossips. Others actively work to destabilize your agenda through disinformation. A well-informed office staff can be a bulwark against rampant rumors. Shower them with praise for handling communications with patience and accuracy.

The Grapevine

Some staff members and the majority of the community are hardwired into the grapevine, which is about as reliable as talking through a tin can with a string, but wildly popular because of the "buzz," the insiderness that's so much juicier than reading a newsletter—no matter how well written. Don't try to root out the grapevine. Find it and use it. If you have detractors or naysayers who stand in front of the school every day like K-Mart greeters, bury them in information. Put them on your pen-pal list and send them newsletters and research papers. Invite them to every meeting. Then if they want to keep rumoring, they'll have to lie to do it. Flooding the airways with your message is the most powerful way to take the juice out of the grapevine.

Cosmopsis

Even if you become the information guru in your district, there will still be days when you simply cannot outrun the incoming tide of communication demands. If this is also a day when you're exhausted or discouraged, you may find yourself standing stock-still for whole minutes, as if you've just emerged from a coma. Your desk is gridlocked with memos and messages so urgent that you want to throw a red blanket over them and call 911. Instead, you're frozen on the spot because you can't conjure up a single gesture that would make a dent in the mound of obligation. So you do nothing.

It's called *cosmopsis*—the cosmic view. It's a paralysis of the body when the mind can't find the reason to act. In the novel, *The End of the Road* by Roland Barth (1967), the main character finds himself stranded on the platform in Penn Station, immobilized because he can't think of any reason to go anywhere, and apparently he can't go anywhere without a reason. His therapist devises an intriguing solution. He can avoid cosmopsis by repeating a popular soda jingle—"Pepsi-Cola hits the spot, big five ounces, that's a lot."

I actually tried it a few times and had a chuckle, which was an improvement in itself. What worked best for me was the Rule of Five. This mind-bogglingly simple technique always gets me unstuck. I tell myself that I can't possibly do everything that's piled before me, but I can do five things and then quit. Five emails, five phone calls, or five memos awaiting reply. Or I say that I'll just work for five minutes and then stop. While I'm working, I repeat over and over, *All progress is progress*. I usually work longer, and do more than the promised five, because I regain emotional control. Next time you can't move or think, try counting to five. Or have a Pepsi and go home early. It will all be waiting for you in the morning—and even more—because the in-box never sleeps.

11

Message in a Bottle

Getting Smarter About Public Relations

- Take a Look: Assessing Your School's Image
- Spit and Polish: PR Projects on a Shoestring
- Pump Up the Volume: Other PR Opportunities
- A Picture and a Thousand Words: Talking School Success

One scorching August afternoon, a weary mother and daughter trekked across the parking lot of the local high school, eager to enroll for the fall semester. They picked their way through a tangle of late-summer construction, skirted temporary barriers, and threaded a maze of dusty corridors. No signs guided them. No volunteers directed their wandering. A series of wrong turns left them stranded on the edge of the football field, where they flagged down a passing staff member. When asked where the registrar might be found, the terse responder offered, "That's not my department," and moved on.

What are the odds that this parent will believe the shiny vinyl banner announcing "Excellence in Education" when she finally stumbles upon the registration hall? I'd put them somewhere between slim and none.

Good principals work hard at selling their schools to a wary community. They labor over newsletters, vision statements, brochures, even bumper stickers. If they're persistent, they may capture a few column inches in the local newspaper. Unfortunately, most of these public relations efforts are about as reliable as a message in a bottle. No matter how well crafted the message, there's no guarantee if or when it will reach its intended audience.

Meanwhile, the school facility itself—buildings, playfields, parking lots, and marquee—broadcasts round-the-clock advertisements about your school, at a volume just shy of a Who concert, to the thousands of people who drive by or drop in every day—the mayor, the mail carrier, alumni, school board members, first-time parents and grandparents. You can stand by and let your school shame you, or harness the energy of your staff to shout a positive message, twenty-four hours a day by learning strategies to polish up your public image.

Take a Look: Assessing Your School's Image

What's the drive-by impression of your campus? Does it shout "proud" or "pathetic"? Does it seem safe or encourage drivers to hit the accelerator? Are the hallways so disheveled and dark that visitors have to feel their way to a light switch? How about your front office? Does it look like a kid-friendly portal, or a dumpster after an earthquake?

To assess your school image, just take a walk, or rather a walk-through, a valuable activity I learned during a School Public Relations Institute. The School Image Walk-Through is a project to assess the positive or negative messages your facility communicates. It allows a team of your staff members to look at your campus as if they were tourists or perspective home buyers. Try to include a teacher; your plant manager; a parent; representatives from classified staff, student government, and campus security; and an administrator on your team. Walk around the school grounds and through the offices. Visit the communal areas and selected classrooms. Use the checklist below to scour the campus for items or areas that send a negative message about your school. Then get to work.

>
> "The voyage of discovery is not in seeking new landscapes but in having new eyes."
> —Marcel Proust

The walk-through should take about an hour. When you're finished, take some time as a team to discuss your impressions. Have a recorder summarize your findings as data to present at faculty, governance, student council, and PTA meetings. Ask for ideas, solutions, volunteers, and suggestions for resources. Then come up with a project plan and time lines. Publish your plan along with an invitation to all interested parties.

>
> "A rock pile ceases to be a rock pile the moment a single man contemplates it, bearing within him the image of a cathedral."
> —Antoine de Saint-Exupéry

THE SCHOOL IMAGE WALK-THROUGH

Area Observed	Assessment	Improvements
CURB APPEAL		
School Name		
Address		
Landscaping		
Litter		
Marquee		
NAVIGATING		
Campus Map		
Building Signs		
Classroom Numbers		
Entrance/Exit Signs		
Procedures for Visiting		
WELCOME MAT		
Visitor Parking		
Main Entrance		
Reception Area		
Visitor Sign-In		
Chairs for Visitors		
General Office Appearance		
Clear Countertops		
FACES AND VOICES		
Nameplates on Desks		
Designated Receptionist		
Prompt and Friendly Greeting		
Multilingual Staff or Translators		

Answering Machine with Current Information		
GETTING TO KNOW US		
Vision Statement		
Trophy Case and Awards		
Historic Photos		
Current Projects		
Student Work Displayed		
PRIDE OF PLACE		
Bulletin Boards and Walls		
Hallways, Floors, and Stairwells		
Restrooms and Drinking Fountains		
Trash Containers		
PARENTS AS PARTNERS		
Parent Resource Table		
Community Bulletin Board		
School Calendar		
Volunteer Badges and Sign-In		
Volunteer Recognition Board		
MEETING SPACES		
Library		
Gymnasium		
Auditorium		
Cafeteria		
Multipurpose Room		
Theatre		
Playing Fields		

Spit and Polish: PR Projects on a Shoestring

With a single walk-through, you can harness the public relations potential of dozens of areas on your campus and trumpet what's great about your school to a much larger audience. Take a look at some of the improvements schools have undertaken after a School Image Walk-Through as a starting point for your own action plan.

- a self-serve information center for parents
- storage closets for volunteers
- a gardening party to landscape the entry walkway
- weekly messages on the marquee
- trash cans painted with the school slogan
- a bulletin board documenting student and family community-service projects
- monthly art displays mixing student and community artists
- supergraphics—colorful numbers and words—identifying each building
- raised gardens behind each classroom
- a drop-off zone to avoid traffic backups on the boulevard
- silhouettes of children painted on the buildings
- murals depicting scenes from local history
- camouflaging the emergency storage bins with trellises
- reminder signs about locking gates to enhance campus security
- entry walls decorated with tiles painted by students and families
- plants and table lamps in the staff lounge
- daily newspaper, parenting magazines, and educational research papers in the waiting area
- lending library for parents of students with special needs
- midday trash and bathroom checks
- dumpsters relocated to the side of the school
- parent notice board at the back gate of the school as well as the front
- portable awnings to create additional outdoor workspace
- "Your tax dollars at work" signs on campus construction projects thanking the community for passing the facilities bond
- longtime residents share their school photos from the past five decades for a School History display

Pump Up the Volume: Other PR Opportunities

After your first walk-through you may notice a general upgrading of class-rooms or the staff lounge, as people discover that everyone benefits from an enhanced environment, especially the people for whom the campus is a home away from home. But one shot won't get the job done. The best school pub-lic relations campaigns use many small iterations of the same message over an extended period of time. Your next goal is to identify as many opportunities as possible to send a well-focused message about the school to anyone who will listen.

This will probably seem easier and more fun if you approach public re-lations as a conversation with your community. Think "information." You have a bumper crop of data, daily anecdotes, and little-known facts about your school, and you're eager to share. The community is interested but un-derinformed. It's a perfect fit. But remember, leadership is not enough. Every staff member is a key player on your public relations team. Help them get involved.

- View every staff member as a public relations ambassador for your school. Work with them to identify the three best things about your school. Post these points of pride on signs around campus and incor-porate them into your newsletter and stationary.

- Get business cards printed for staff members with the three best things included in the text. Every time they give away their card, they're spreading a positive message about your school.

- Use your marquee to flash school news items, not just meeting dates. Ask the school image team to write up a dozen short, positive items for your sign. Frequent sign changes convey a dynamic image and keep the public informed.

- Schedule monthly school tours so prospective parents and community members can meet you and visit classes in session. Let your staff know how proud you are to "show off." Everyone spruces up for company, so tours create a built-in maintenance schedule for your walk-through goals.

- Commission a website for your school. This is easier than it sounds since many websites are designed and maintained by computer wiz-ards who still order Happy Meals at McDonald's. Encourage or stipend a faculty member to take on the website project. No takers? Talk to parents or get your school adopted by an ad agency. Many of them have pro bono work in their business plans. You might entice a group of PR students at the local university to design your school image as part of their course requirements.

- Redesign your enrollment cards to include email addresses. Create an email grapevine to inform parents, teachers, and community partners. This list can provide reminders, good news, or rapid information in a crisis. Remember that all families don't have email, so distribute printed versions at the same time, to avoid creating an electronic in-crowd.

- Place an inexpensive ad in the local paper thanking the community after a successful fund-raiser or community effort. Sign it from the principal and the staff.

- Send a personal note to all entering kindergarteners, welcoming them to the school. This makes a huge impression on new families.

- If you have exactly zero dollars for facilities upgrades, such as weeding or gardens, tap into an adult volunteer organization or contact kids who need to do community service—Boy Scouts or Girl Scouts for a start.

- Identify a limited effort that will have a big visual impact—a small area that faces the street or the front entrance. Add color with plants in pots, a new coat of paint on the front door, a plastic banner, or just a rolling chalkboard covered with bright paper, a simple greeting, and student art.

> *"Even though you're on the right track, you'll get run over if you just sit there."*
>
> —Will Rogers

A Picture and a Thousand Words: Talking School Success

Now that your school site and staff are working overtime to project a positive image, seize the moment. Run through your daybook or palm pilot and re-think each meeting or appointment as a publicity event. Jot down one message you'd like the audience to take home, then figure out how to work it into the agenda or your spontaneous remarks. Never go to a meeting unprepared.

I don't have to tell you that school bashing is both easy and fashionable, but there's a lot to be proud of in public education. Use every opportunity to share positive data. Cite a national trend, then personalize it with anecdotes to show how your school is doing compared to schools nationwide. Check the "Know Your Resources" section of Chapter 12, "Knowledge Is Power," for excellent sources on statistics and trends such as the following:

- Thousands of severely disabled students who used to be banished to separate sites and segregated with other disabled students are included in regular classrooms.
- Impressive amounts of technology have been integrated into classrooms all the way down to kindergarten.
- There has been a steady increase in AP and honors participation for a broader spectrum of students.
- The general curriculum is more rigorous, content standards are replacing norm-referenced testing, and children are safer at school than anywhere else in their lives.

Talk regularly with members of the real estate board, chamber of commerce, or Rotary. Many of these organizations are happy to have guest speakers at their meetings, especially someone like an administrator who has on-the-ground information about the schools and larger issues in the community. Put members of the media on your email list. Make a habit of sending them a least one press release or update per month. Keep them informed of all upcoming events, even if they don't cover the story or respond. If nothing else, you're counteracting the negative news they hear on other education issues.

Proud to Lead

And last, but definitely not least, while touting everything that's good and growing about your school, don't forget to give credit where credit is due—to yourself. Most adults think of school administrators as faceless, nameless bureaucrats, responsible for, but unresponsive to, the problems in public education. Put your humility aside and use your best teaching skills to help your community get to know you as an educational leader. Share your qualifications, your range of teaching experiences, your leadership training, areas of expertise, publications, awards, and fellowships. In other words, give them the information they need to appreciate your personal contibution to student achievement. Then talk specifically about the demands of your job, the spectrum of responsibilities that you face in a single day, and the joy—above all the joy. That's a message your community can never hear too often.

12
Knowledge Is Power
Getting Smarter About Professional Growth

- Know Your Resources
- Know the Contract
- Know the Drills
- Know the Law

If you are a typical school administrator, you've probably been in school eighteen years, three months, five days, and twenty-six minutes. Even if you're on a provisional credential or waiver, you have more credits than God. So why on earth would I suggest that you squeeze one more obligation—professional growth—into your maximum-occupancy daybook?

Survival. You have to get smarter to survive. One out of three principals leave their positions involuntarily. Read *fired*. They're "serving at the pleasure of the board" one day—job hunting the next. If you didn't see the word *tenure* in your contract, don't even think about due process, and don't expect career guidance or a constructive explanation from your boss, unless the phrase "not a good fit" is enlightening to you. Superintendents don't like firing people any more than you do, so your exit interview may be a brief encounter of the tersest kind.

So how do you learn what you need to know to survive? Teachers' surveys are a good place to start. When teachers were asked to list the mistakes that administrators make, they ranked poor human relations right at the top. That was followed by poor communication, failure to lead, snap judgments, lack of knowledge about curriculum and instruction, forgetting what it's like to be a teacher, and—in a swift reversal of thinking—failure to hold staff accountable. Somewhere down the list was interrupting instruction with public-address-system announcements!

You might be inclined to stagger right out of that paragraph and into the arms of a headhunter. The reality is that most of those failings can be addressed through professional development, but not if you're Velcroed to your desk. You have to get out and get trained. Right now you're probably making a mental list of the reasons why you don't attend leadership workshops, much less take off for three days—seventy-two whole hours—to attend a conference in another city. Most principals feel the same way. When asked, "Professional development—why not you?" the majority answer, "No time." "Not a good use of my time." "Not an ethical use of my time." Here's the most intriguing response. "Fear of exposure." Some principals worry that learning in any form is an admission that they don't know everything—a pretty scary attitude in a profession that touts lifelong learning.

Granted, some administrators err in the opposite direction, leaping on each new trend like it's the last helicopter out of Saigon. Their staffs have lived through management-by-wandering, restructuring, whole-school reform, shared decision making, site-based management, Zen and the art of lunchroom supervision, tipping points, and the Way of the Warrior. Reduced to the status of crash-test dummies, teachers slap their foreheads in unison and say, "Oh, God, he's been to another conference."

But most administrators undertrain themselves, especially in areas that directly affect their performance as school leaders, which directly affects their survival in the profession. It's not totally their fault. In the past decade the job has quadrupled in scope while training opportunities have lagged far behind. The Clinton administration acknowledged this gap in the 2001 School Leadership Initiative, which proposed spending $40 million to establish much-needed regional training centers for principals. Many private foundations have also adopted principal training as their *cause celebre*. Help may be on the way, but you need support every day, on a moment's notice, to wrestle with tough legal questions and ethical dilemmas, while reinventing learning on a shoestring budget.

The question is, Do you want to keep your job? If the answer is yes, put self-development on your To Do list and get it done, because when you perform better, the whole organization improves, and that reflects well on you. Get smarter and share the wealth.

Know Your Resources

You probably thought teaching was draining, until you moved into the principal's office. Now you're the go-to person for hundreds of people, but where do you turn for answers? Smart principals tear themselves away long enough to stay ahead of the avalanche of new mandates and research on teaching and learning. They read, surf the Net, cruise through a conference, or have drinks with colleagues, all in an effort to stay current.

You don't have to leave town—or even your office—to get smarter. With a phone, fax, and computer, you can set up a self-service principal's academy simply by tapping into a broad array of professional organizations and educational websites. Start with these.

Professional Organizations

- National Association of Elementary School Principals
  www.naesp.org
- National Association of Secondary School Principals
  www.nassp.org
- National Middle School Association   www.nmsa.org
- National High School Association   www.nhsa.org
- Association for Supervision and Curriculum Design   www.ascd.org

Professional Development Resources

- National Board for Professional Teaching Standards
  www.nbpts.org
- National Staff Development Council   www.nsdc.org
- Professional Academies   www.aapsga.org/academies
- National Partnership for Excellence and Accountability in Teaching
  www.npeat.org

Internet Research

As the leader of an educational enterprise, you should be able to link your vision to the research that distinguishes best practices from a multitude of other interesting ideas. Staff and community are impressed when you explain student success in the context of the geography of the brain, or assure them that reading aloud to children is the single greatest predictor that they will become readers. The problem is that you scarcely have time to be a reader, much less a researcher.

Don't panic. ERIC to the rescue. ERIC, the Educational Resources Information Center (www.askeric.org), is the premiere, one-stop resource for any topic in education—concisely presented, low jargon, high content, with excellent bibliographies and weblinks. So if you're looking for grants, preparing a proposal, planning staff development, designing a parent survey, updating handbooks, or writing a school safety plan, this is the place for you. ERIC has clearinghouses on assessment, special education, management, early childhood, parent training, technology, service learning, standards, and dozens of other topics. The format is so accessible and the website so user-friendly that you may become an after-hours research junkie. Worse things could happen to you.

If you need to spruce up a grant application with up-to-date statistics, try the National Center for Education Statistics (www.ed.gov/NCES), or THOMAS—U. S. Congress on the Internet (www.thomas.loc.gov). To keep abreast of the national education trends, browse Education Week (www. edweek.org) online. Ten minutes on this site will help you keep your oar in professional conversations, and prepare your for the next wave of reform before it swamps you.

Know the Contract

I may be one of the few administrators to earn a grievance before becoming principal. I was teaching middle school humanities when I was selected for my first principalship. It was only March, but the superintendent's idea of an interesting transition was for me to teach in morning, run home, and suit up—literally, and head for my new school, to attend or lead meetings. Not exactly trial by fire, since many in the community were thrilled to have a willing principal after a year with no one at the helm.

However, enthusiasm was not universal. At the end of one particularly long day, a fourth-grade teacher confronted me in the office. She stood about as close as a person can and still be considered Western, and in a voice as forceful as a tantrum she announced, "We didn't have a principal for a year, and we did just fine." It was a welcome of sorts. I met up with her a week later, and this time I was on the business end of a grievance. It seems I'd ignored the local rituals around combination classes, and earned my first Scarlet G. I had a lot to learn.

I've been told that the boss' copy of the union contract should be as dog-eared as the shop foreman's, and that's good advice. Unfortunately, reading a contract is about as interesting as watching paint dry. If you're staring at a two-hundred-page monster, you may be tempted to just chuck it, and take your chances. But that can mean grievances, litigation, or at least mild social embarrassment. Your resident contract wonk can torpedo an entire staff development plan with a single obscure clause from Appendix A. If done in public, it undermines your credibility with the staff.

So spare yourself the grief. Take time before you're under fire to red-flag the explosive paragraphs in your contract. If you're not sure where the hot buttons are, sit down with your union representative to review critical local topics—what's meaningless to one staff may create fireworks with another. Enlist the rep's aid in working out plans to avoid unintended confrontations. But don't stop there. Call a colleague or the administrator in charge of human resources—whoever handles grievances—to get another perspective. Ask which sections of the contract are most frequently contested, misinterpreted, or hopelessly muddled. Then you can start to devise strategies to handle thorny contract issues.

Hot Topics in Teacher Contracts

Settle down with your teacher contract, a yellow highlighter, and a block of Post-it Notes, and comb the table of contents. Highlight, annotate, and label the contract until it looks like your favorite cookbook. Indexing your copy helps you cut to the chase in contract discussions. Here are some items to start with.

Location, Location, Location. Teachers want to know where they will be working. Which school, which department, which room. Some have been living in the same space for decades—there's a microwave, refrigerator, and stereo system to prove it. What you consider reorganizing may feel like an eviction notice to even the most cooperative teacher. So scan the parts of the contract that cover transfers, minimum square footage, room assignments, shared space, and roving. If you move a teacher from one wing to another, or even next door, you may have to provide movers, release time, and additional pay. If you know the contract, you can offer assistance up front to ease the discomfort of dislocation.

Teaching Assignments. Responsibility for assigning teachers varies widely from district to district. You may have complete control or be the last to know, depending on contract language. Watch for time lines, seniority, special credential requirements, and the distribution of hardships, such as combination classes.

Evaluation and Dismissal of Teachers. Two words to keep in mind on this topic—time lines and documents.

The contracts I've read are loaded with time lines for evaluating staff, and woefully short on expectations for performance. So you need to share your expectations, and explain how you'll observe and evaluate teachers. But whatever you do, watch those dates. Write them in your daybook, put them in a tickler file, tattoo them on your forehead if necessary. Whatever it takes, do it. Because if you miss a time line by fifteen seconds, a lunatic is considered satisfactory by default, and you have to start all over. The documents? Use this simple guide: if it's not written down, you didn't do it. For all the details, see Chapter 9, "Pruning in the Minefield."

More Contract Topics You Need to Know

- Maximum class size or case load, exceptions, and waivers
- Compensation for training, committee work, supervision
- Workday, hours, breaks, and lunch periods. What does "the end of the professional day" mean?
- Transfer policy, especially time lines and rights of transferring teachers
- Seniority for summer school positions, stipends, and overtime
- Sexual harassment
- Confidentiality
- Child abuse reporting requirements

When you get all finished with the teachers' contract, start on the one for your classified staff. It's equally technical and equally important.

Remember, contracts are written by committees, which may explain why entire sections read like pig Latin. If you're not sure what a clause means, don't rely on one person's translation. Call the union president for an interpretation, then call the head of your administrative negotiating team, and see if the two stories match. You may be the first person to stumble upon a real conundrum. Let the lawyers work it out and tell staff you'll get back to them with an answer as soon as possible.

> *"If you fail to prepare, you are preparing to fail."*
> —Benjamin Franklin

Know the Drills

Every day that I was principal, I would send a pathetic plea skyward. "Please, God, if there's an earthquake, let it happen after four-thirty." The responsibility for nine hundred lives in a catastrophe rested in the pit of my stomach like brick, and I was grateful each day that the seismologists had nothing to report. I suspect that all principals say some version of this prayer to fend off natural or human disasters. Prayer is good—but planning is a must.

It's important to say that schools are relatively safe places. In fact, kids are safer in school than almost any other place in their lives. But having said that, crisis prevention and crisis response are two critical areas of your professional development that just can't wait. Novice principals don't have immunity from random acts of violence, and seasoned veterans can't count on that fact that nothing has happened so far.

So at the risk of scaring yourself silly, close your eyes and imagine gunfire at noon, at your school, then let the scene roll. What would you do first? Please don't say run toward the shots, since the entire school depends on your leadership in a crisis. Does your staff know the code and procedure for a lockdown? Who's on your crisis team? How well do they know their roles? Who contacts the police? The superintendent? Who's assigned to handle the media when they descend? Has that person been trained in the ABCs of crisis communication? What happens when parents arrive in a panic? Do they know about your evacuation and reunion plans? If you don't know the answers to these questions, you should be (1) worried, (2) motivated, or (3) looking for another job.

Serious events such as shootings, bomb threats, hostage situations, airplane crashes, or toxic chemical spills are rare, but they require quick and preplanned responses. A comprehensive plan for dealing with any crisis includes:

- A crisis response team with clearly delineated duties
- A plan for locking down and evacuating the school
- A plan for notifying and coordinating with police, district officials, government agencies, and other proper authorities
- A plan for notifying parents quickly
- A media/communication strategy
- Counselors available to deal with students in the aftermath of a traumatic event

If you don't have an updated Comprehensive School Safety Plan, assemble a school safety group, and ask for help. Call your district school safety office or risk-management person; talk to your local police or fire department; go on the Internet for dozens of how-to articles; and call the mental health agencies in your community to explore posttraumatic support in the event of a crisis, including the death of a student by suicide, accident, or violence. Contact your county office of education or the State Department of Education Safe Schools Division. Read *Early Warning, Timely Response: A Guide to Safe Schools,* published by the U. S. Department of Education and the U. S. Department of Justice. When your written plan is complete, schedule drills throughout the year, practicing until students and staff know their roles and can perform them with confidence.

The most horrifying school tragedy is the homegrown variety, when students turn on their classmates or teachers. So once your crisis plans are in place, focus your energy where it will do the most good—on your students. Work with them to create a climate of tolerance. Provide appropriate educational and counseling services to students who are emotionally or socially challenged. Involve students in making decisions about school policies and programs. Monitor every inch of your campus to ensure that it is clean and safe, so students feel valued and respected.

> *One of the true tests of leadership is the ability to recognize a problem before it becomes an emergency."*
> —Arnold Glasow

Know the Law

Do you know when to Skelly and when to refrain? Can you turn your auditorium over to the local church on Sundays? How about the Boy Scouts? Do you know when a gun is not a firearm, and why it matters? Maybe. Maybe not. After all, if you'd wanted a career in quid pro quo, you would have gone to law school. You chose education, and now it's hard to tell the difference.

A nationwide survey of principals recently indicated that they're altering or completely eliminating basic programs and activities for fear of lawsuits. Field trips, athletic activities, after-school events, even the lyrics for choral concerts are scrutinized with the eye of a circuit court judge. Twenty per cent of the principals said they spend five to ten hours per week avoiding litigation. Six percent reported a depressing ten to twenty hours devoted to fending off legal eagles.

But if you ignore the law, you're liable to find yourself staring down the barrel of a due-process hearing or playing pen pals with someone whose name ends in JD. The first words out of your mouth may be, "Who knew?" Well, it turns out that it's your job to know, and ignorance is no excuse. With litigation on the rise, principals must speak school law fluently, so let's start at the very beginning.

The Education Code

Your state's *Education Code* is the how-to guide for schools, covering everything from early kindergarten admission to seat belts on buses, with sexual harassment, hospital instruction, and homeless families in between. You don't need to memorize it, but have it within arm's reach. You can get the three-pound, fine-print version, or find a website where you can execute searches by topic to save time. In California there's one website that carries all state codes at a glance—building, fish and game, penal—as well as how to expel a gun-toting student.

My personal lifesaver in legal matters is *Between a Rock and a Hard Place: Law for School Administrators* by Lillian Lee Port (2000). I also had a brilliant colleague, Phil Cott, a lawyer-turned-principal, who knew the law and was never afraid to wade into a battle—especially a war of words. I called him for coaching and courage. If you're not lucky enough to have a Cott in your corner, here are several handy websites that can help you in a pinch:

- Education Law Web Guide   www.findlaw.com
- National School Board Association   www.nsba.org
- U. S. Codes   http://law.house.gov/usc.html
- Federal Regulations   http://www.access.gpo.gov/nara/cfr /index.html

Board Policy

This is your local bible—usually a binder the size of a telephone book and just about as fascinating. It's a trove of information and procedures—field trips, transcripts, dress codes, homework, liability, even when you must do the flag salute—things that you need to know to stay out of trouble. Unfortunately, much of it is written in language that begs for subtitles. As a result, few people read it, including the board members who preside over it. But help is just a phone call away. There's a person in the central office who tends to policy

> *"The price of power is responsibility for the common good."*
>
> —Winthrop Aldrich

issues—try student services. As a new principal I was coached by Rick Bagley, who speaks policy fluently, and as a bonus, wrote blazing letters peppered with six-digit citations to scofflaws who were making a misery of my life. Locate your policy binder and local guru for the help you deserve.

Special Education Law

Remember when IDEA was something brilliant you had while shaving or taking a shower? Well, think again. IDEA is a complex set of federal regulations that provide protection for persons with disabilities in school settings—special education. Providing special education services is a huge responsibility that some principals ignore or delegate. They're conspicuously absent when IEP invitations are being passed out, and think the 504 is a freeway. But you can't afford to be casual about this topic, because what you don't know about special education law can disadvantage students, impede learning, enrage parents, exhaust your staff, and cost you your job. I can put it no other way. My advice? Embrace IDEA and recognize its potential as a powerful tool for helping students.

There are lots of ways to get smarter about special education. As with so many other topics, I learned on the job. Some IEPs at my school looked like senate subcommittee hearings, with as many as twelve experts, advocates, specialists, service providers, and school staff huddled in a stuffy room, discussing goals and services. Some meetings were wildly successful—truly a team effort. Others were agony, and months or even years later, we'd have a grim reunion at a due-process hearing. Along the way, I learned enough to be appointed codirector of special education for our district.

If you're starting from scratch, read the parent rights booklet that must be offered at every IEP meeting. Check websites, go to conferences, and keep asking questions. Then train yourself to think like a diagnostician and document like a lawyer.

There are thousands of websites, public and private, government and advocate, devoted to special education issues and laws. Sites sponsored by parent organizations are excellent sources for learning about cutting-edge interventions and what's-in-the-pipeline research. Here's a sampling.

Office of Civil Rights   www.ed.gov/offices/OCR

Office of Special Education   www.ed.gov/offices/OSERS/OSEP

IDEA Practices U.S. Department of Education
www.ideapractices.org

National Council on Disabilities   www.ncd.gov

Center for Law and Education   www.cleweb.org

Center for Special Education Advocacy   www.cseadvocacy.com
Education Law Center   www.elc-pa.org

Student Discipline

School discipline means one thing these days—providing a safe campus. Not just gun-knife-drug-safe. You must actively work to protect students against harassment, bullying, gender discrimination, and hate crimes related to race, ethnicity, or sexual orientation. In short, you must vigorously suppress any activity that creates an environment so hostile that it interferes with learning. And all your disciplinary efforts must fall within the guidelines of your state education code and local board policy. Since the state code is subject to change by the legislature, find a website for legislative updates, and have one of your support staff download it periodically, highlighting any new education bills that could affect life on your campus.

Here are the basic guidelines for creating an effective discipline policy. It should be a written document that is clear and well publicized. The consequences must be applied in a manner that is progressive, flexible, and consistent. There are dozens of articles on the Web to guide you in forming your approach to student behavior. Some systems consist of positive statements or "great expectations" for students. Others list the "do nots." In either case, the policy needs to be a readable and well-designed statement, deposited into the hands of every student and explicitly discussed with them. Most schools issue a student handbook or send the policy home on a form with a parent signature tear-off. Without a written policy, broadly communicated, students are ignorant of the rules and discipline seems unfair.

Fairness also requires that discipline be progressive. If a student with a perfect discipline record gets caught stealing CDs from backpacks, you can't request expulsion. You must start with appropriate consequences for first offenders. Second-offense discipline and interventions increase in severity. In disciplinary proceedings, including suspensions and expulsions, the school must show that all feasible means of correction have failed to bring about the desired behavior in the student before serious penalties are imposed. You can't go from zero to sixty with students unless they commit a major offense—such as having firearms on campus, selling drugs, sexual assault, or serious injury to another. If your district has zero-tolerance policies, have your policy expert or legal counsel explain exactly what that means. You don't want to make the front page of the local newspaper for an Advil expulsion.

If a student is in special education or has a 504 plan, discipline with caution, and always check the law. There is nothing in IDEA that restricts schools from disciplining students with disabilities; however, you must be sure that the unacceptable behavior is not a manifestation of the disability before you can impose serious disciplinary measures. For example, when an emotionally disturbed student uses threatening language, it may violate your discipline policy, but if it is a manifestation of his disability, normal consequences would be inappropriate. It is then the duty of the IEP team to provide services that would help that student understand school rules and comply to the best of his ability, including a behavior contract, behavior modification, counseling, or a social skills class. If an IEP team determines that the misconduct is not a manifestation of the student's disability, then students may be subject to the regular discipline code of consequences, provided that they continue to receive all their IEP services.

If you're starting from scratch or revising an existing discipline policy, make it a collaborative effort with teachers, parents, administrators, and even students joining in the discussion. This may seem laborious but it kills a flock of birds with one stone. Discussion creates awareness. Parents who create the policy are more likely to back you up on a tough call. Teachers who have a say in crafting the rules are more likely to be consistent in their application. The final document reflects community norms about how students should behave, and broadcasts your efforts to maintain a safe, violence-free school.

Divorce, Custody, and Parent Disputes

Nearly a third of the children in our schools live with only one parent, sometimes caught in long and acrimonious custody battles. Your school may be named in cocustody agreements as the hub where disputants cross paths, casting you in the role of referee. Elaborate pickup and drop-off arrangements get the judicial seal, leaving you to sort out who's on the emergency card, who gets report cards, and whether a joint parent conference will need an armed guard or only a mediator.

If a custody dispute arises at your school, protect your staff by having the parents come to your office, a conference room, or any suitable location away from classrooms. Insulate students from the immediate conflict, and then deescalate the situation using active listening and your best social skills to calm the adults. Don't try to resolve the conflict—that's why we have courts. Be evenhanded with both parties—never take sides. Say as little as possible, since you may be quoted or misquoted in court documents.

Always ask for a current copy of the custody agreement to keep on file, then scan the document for the basic agreement. Here are terms you need to know:

- Joint custody means joint physical and legal custody.
- Sole physical custody means that a child will reside with and under the supervision of one parent. The court controls visitation.
- Joint physical custody means that each parent shall have significant periods of physical custody.
- Sole legal custody means that one parent shall have the right and responsibility to make decisions relating to health, education, and welfare of the child.
- Joint legal custody means that both parents shall share the right and responsibility to make decisions relating to health, education, and welfare of the child.

If the court language is too spare to be practical, send the parents back to court for clarification. In all cases, the natural parent of a child has the right to all school records, even if they are denied any form of custody.

Parents sometimes ask teachers to write letters that comment on (1) their fitness as parent, (2) the unfitness of the other parent, (3) the impact of the divorce on the child's performance in school. I had one unfortunate teacher hustled off in a taxi to testify at a custody hearing, subpoenaed by a parent hoping to score points by putting her under oath. Remind staff that the court will request additional educational information if it sees fit, but in the absence of a court request, it is wise to refrain from making written or oral statements that can fuel a custody dispute.

More Legal Advice

Research, preparation, and experience are the keys to mastering most administrative challenges. But even if you have been in the business for decades, there will still be times when you're faced with a situation that smells like trouble. Don't ignore your nose or your gut. Even if you have to excuse yourself from a meeting, and make a call on your cell phone from a pay toilet, take care of yourself—ask an expert. There's someone at the central office that handles legal issues. If your district is large, you may have an in-house legal division. If not, someone at the assistant superintendent level is the liaison between your district and a law firm that's retained to solve problems. It's his or her job to keep your fanny out of hot water, and the district out of court, so they have a vested interest in pointing out the legal land mines. But they can't help you if you don't sound the alarm, so get to know your legal expert, do your homework, and never think that your questions are too trivial to ask. An entire case can hang on the stroke of your pen. Ask, ask, ask.

Another great source of legal advise is your county office of education, which has a staff of lawyers and ed-code jockeys who eat and drink jurisprudence. There are divisions for special education, discipline, enrollment and permits, child welfare, as well as human resources. Try to get your hands on a county directory and get to know the players. Don't be afraid to cold-call— county staffs are well trained and service oriented.

Finally, there may be times when you want a second opinion, or you feel too vulnerable discussing a problem with the central office, for fear that it will reflect badly on you, or become fodder for the next performance evaluation. If you belong to a professional organization for administrators, you may be entitled to a free consultation with an attorney who specializes in school law. Call the member benefits person to access this assistance. An hour on the phone with an education lawyer can ease your mind, or at least give you clearer answers. In the game of leadership, you can never learn too much.

13

A Mentor a Day

Getting Smarter About Personal Growth

- Mentor as Research Resource
- Mentor as Think Tank
- Mentor as Mirror of Reality
- Mentor as Personal Cheerleader
- Mentor as Rescue 911
- Mentor as Mental Health Monitor

It's no secret that university programs for aspiring administrators utterly fail to capture the reality and complexity of the workplace we call school. Administrative credentialing programs are notoriously bad—theoretical, vague, and unwilling to address the grueling nature of life as a school leader. After two years of classes and thousands of dollars, most principals could drive a truck through the gap between what they learned in their credential program and what they need to know in their first week on the job.

Without a mentor, novice and not-so-novice administrators stumble about in the vast gray landscape of leadership, make unnecessary mistakes, feel inadequate, and suffer. Sometimes experience is their best teacher, and they grow strong and confident. More often the early years are such a nonstop anxiety festival that many promising leaders abandon the profession before they ever experience their true potential.

To staunch the leadership drain that is reaching crisis proportions, local, state, and federal agencies are creating mentor programs for principals. They recognize that principals learn best when assistance programs are based on the specific circumstances in which they are working. Support needs to be delivered to their doors and tailored to the crisis of the moment. Mentors seem to be the answer—assembling an army of credible mentors is the challenge. I call it the Have Scar Tissue, Will Travel project. And it's not just for newborn principals. Experienced administrators sign up for mentors, too, if only for the company of a survivor who speaks leadership in shorthand.

To fill this need, retired administrators are lured off the golf links to share their knowledge and experience. Business leaders teach crossover skills to help principals survive the budget wars. In desperation, some districts recruit sitting principals who already have their hands full to coach principals who still need their training wheels.

> "There is no more noble occupation in the world than to assist another human being—to help someone succeed."
> —Alan Loy McGinnis

Mentor Shopping

If you don't have a mentor, maybe you should be in the market. If you shop carefully and choose well, you can add years to your career. Good mentors are caring leaders who derive a deep satisfaction from encouraging development in others. They're big-picture people who can see farther down your road than you may ever dream of going, and pinpoint the skills you need to get there. Great mentors give freely without the expectation of return.

Having a bad mentor is like calling 911, then being run over by the ambulance when it arrives. Bad mentors are morale busters. They sap your limited strength by setting unrealistically high goals or generating so many suggestions for "growth" that you feel like you're trying to suck air through a straw from under a pile of manure. It's hard to grow when you're buried alive. And there are mentors who are so insecure that they diminish the accomplishments of their protégés to retain their own stature. Dump these obstructionists—and keep on searching.

What makes a mentorship work? Trust. Respect for knowledge. Sympathetic points of view on pedagogy. A critical element is a common understanding of the day-to-day work. The last thing you need after a crushing vox populi defeat in your governance council is a sermon from an ivory-tower theorist who couldn't construct a master schedule at gunpoint.

If you go mentor shopping, it's best to look outside your district. Try a university, neighboring district, support group, professional organization, or the local administrator's retirement village. If no one in the vicinity fits the bill, try e-mentoring or use the phone to erase the miles between you and a cherished colleague who's moved away. You may even start pen-pal-ing with someone whose writing or thinking you admire. Using an outsider eliminates the fear of being judged. You don't want to play True Confessions only to be skewered with your own quotes in an evaluation conference.

The Heimlich Maneuver and Other Mentor Skills

Good mentors can save your life, or at least your sanity. They can provide a touch of humor at the end of a lousy day or talking points for a tough meeting. Grizzled mentors have anecdotes that make your worst experience look like a school picnic. Most are dedicated enough to join you out on the ledge and tell you their horror stories until you're ready to come back in. And they're loaded with practical advice that can save you hours of work and help you sleep at night. In addition, your mentor can function in a variety of helpful roles.

Mentor as Research Resource

Try to land a mentor who's smarter than you in the critical areas where you want to grow. If your focus is assessment, you need reliable tools and a clear explanation that you can share with parents and staff. A good mentor can deliver. If your community is poised to revolt against standardized tests, what's a research-based way to support

> *"How do I work? I grope."*
> —Albert Einstein

them, and still reassure board members that your students are mastering the standards? Mentor on speed-dial.

The best mentors have names, facts, and research findings at their fingertips, to guide your growth in that "I-just-happen-to-know" or "I-remember-reading" way that doesn't make you feel like an idiot. They give you shortcuts to the next level of expertise, a trove of data, or the most concise, accessible research on best practices. And within the privacy of your relationship, you're free to puzzle, struggle with ideas, and reject practices, without an audience.

Mentor as Think Tank

Closing your office door once or twice a month to meet with your mentor can be your own personal think tank where you can let down your guard. This is the time to question the status quo and think of outrageous alternatives. You can be spontaneous and intuitive without fueling the rumor mill or having to defend a half-baked idea at a public meeting. The tank is the place to examine your core values or road test an important presentation to the community. In that same spirit, a good mentor will question you, push your thinking, and be a consistent voice asking, "Have you thought about . . . ?" or "Do you have any data to support that?"

Mentor as Mirror of Reality

The greatest gift of a mentor is to reframe your struggles as evidence of your strength. From your vantage point, the job feels like excavating with a dental pick. You're too tired or daunted by the mountain of what must be done to notice evidence of progress, even if it's right under your nose. A mentor can collect data, and identify inobtrusive measures to help you assess your impact. On a walk through the building, an outsider can pick up the tone of the school, or provide valuable *before* and *after* pictures that capture specific improvements. If the halls used to ring with teachers yelling, and now you can hear kids, that's progress. If the classroom doors were locked, and now some stand open, that's a change. A mentor puts stars on your chart.

There are times when principals find themselves in a fight to the death, defending a bridge they never even meant to cross, much less die on. Somebody gets under your skin, or hurls a gauntlet in public, and the next thing you know, your neurosis has you in a half nelson and won't let go. You're out of control. A good mentor will tell you when you need a time out and when to throw in the towel. If your relationship is solid, you'll listen. You might even be grateful for permission to lose gracefully. A really skilled mentor can help craft a win-win situation. If you're under the wing of someone that gifted, take notes!

Mentor as Personal Cheerleader

An administrator's job is singularly lacking in praise or plaudits. Even if you are a superprincipal, what you do well is more likely to elicit yawns than flowers. And much of your best work is so subtle or politically sensitive that it can't be freely discussed. But you can share your triumph with a mentor and get that pat on the back that you deserve.

If you suffer from the need to be perfect, you may be utterly blind to your own successes. Rather than being encouraged, you obsess on what you could have done better, and you might lose heart. Again, a mentor can

> *"Accept the challenges so that you can feel the exhilaration of victory."*
>
> —George S. Patton

catalogue your progress, and do a compare and contrast to demonstrate how much you've grown.

If you can't find a mentor, set up a support group of two or three other people who understand your job well enough to appreciate your efforts and give good feedback. Stay away from gripe sessions. They just tend to bring everyone down.

Mentor as Rescue 911

Sometimes a mentor's biggest contribution is to keep you away from sharp objects and third-story windows. Depression and despair are realities in school administration. They're temporary—but not a pretty sight. In extreme situations, you may find yourself in a fight-or-flight mode, having totally lost your perspective.

Thus, it is critically important that you find someone with whom you can be your worst self and still feel safe. I was exceptionally lucky in this regard. My mentor, Paul Heckman, had the unflappable air of man who knew his way around disappointment. I could curse and cry and he didn't bat an eye. Once I was over the worst of it, I wanted to get back on course quickly and he was always ready for problem solving. He was also blessed with a sterling sense of humor—a true bonus—since nearly every situation has its humorous aspect, but it takes an outsider to help you see it. It's a real gift to have a mentor who can dislodge a lunatic guffaw from your throat a scant thirty minutes after you'd seriously considered taking a long walk off a short pier.

Mentor as Mental Health Monitor

Leadership brings out the best and the worst in all of us. Stress, isolation, criticism, and working under the constant pressure of time lines are staples of the job. When two or more of those conditions coincide, you may become dysfunctional without a clue to why you fell apart. Childhood demons that you thought you left behind with your high school yearbook can spur your neurosis into a full gallop when your hands are nowhere near the reins.

For example, making tough decisions such as changing teaching assignments can tap directly into your need to be liked, and you may find yourself pulling punches, procrastinating, or waiting for a crisis to force your hand. While a good mentor can tell you when your emotional or psychological baggage is getting in your way, it's not the mentor's role to provide therapy. If you plan to stay in the leadership game, you may find it helpful to meet with a counselor, therapist, or spiritual advisor when the going gets very tough.

Returning the Favor

If you have been a principal for a while, you've gained some valuable knowledge. For example, you know that you should never eat the cafeteria's corn dogs, no matter how hungry you are. Never think Monday will be uneventful, just because you spent all day Sunday in your office catching up. You know how to get extra custodial time and how to get emergency supplies before open house. There's a novice principal somewhere in your town who would love to talk with you. Offer your services as an occasional mentor, so you can help a grateful colleague through the rough spots, and have the thrill of realizing how much you really know.

14
Living Well Is the Best Revenge
Getting Smarter About Managing Stress

- Simple Pleasures
- Feed the Machine
- Thoreau.com
- Is This Hard?
- Read All About It

- Enough Is Enough
- Photo Safari
- Applause, Applause
- Houdini
- Clean Thoughts on a Dirty Wall

Stress is not a modern invention, and it certainly isn't a plague exclusive to school administrators. But if you're a harried principal—and show me one who isn't—even the most mundane day offers dozens of opportunities to boost your stress quotient. Consider the firing squad you could face on any given day—angry parents, passive aggressive teachers, clueless school board members, and sadly, students with guns. Now throw in a host of ethical dilemmas with unclear answers, and the maddening Monday-morning demise of your only Xerox machine. When all is said and done, the opportunities for anxiety, frustration, and long-distance burden bearing are truly dazzling.

It seems like contemporary principals determined to reduce stress at work would need an intravenous drip of Valium or a live-in guru, neither of which is covered by the benefits package. So how do administrators handle stress? An increasing number do a Darwin. They evolve themselves right out of the job—polish up their resumes, slap "Consultant" behind their names, and head for the sweet green hills of early retirement. It's survival of the fittest.

The rest simply roll out of bed, force-march their groggy brains through the latest To Do list, steel their nerves, hit the campus, switch themselves onto autopilot, and work flat out until they slump into their cars and head home. Riding shotgun along with the bulging briefcase is a load of stress so voluminous and lively that it should be subject to the seatbelt laws. Unless you have a very long, very pleasant commute, it's still kicking when you cut the engine. Here's the downside of stockpiling stress until you get home.

- Some days that won't be until ten-thirty or eleven at night. Then it takes hours to unwind. The other option—collapse into bed, sleep badly, and wake up exhausted.
- You walk through the door, swan-dive into a vat of anything alcoholic, and anesthetize yourself. Your brief opportunity for exercise, reading, gardening, sports, or socializing is squandered because you're in a light coma.
- Your roommate, partner, or spouse runs the danger of becoming your designated dumpster. The few hours available for your relationship are preempted by reruns of your lousy day.
- You get hooked on late-night television as an escape, because it makes no demands.
- You stop going home altogether and become a registered workaholic. Twenty-four-seven is your middle name. People can't remember your first name because they never see you.

It's not a pretty picture, but it's pretty accurate. So you need an arsenal of weapons to combat the negative effects of people and events that annoy, anger, wound, and confound you on a daily basis. Rule number one: Don't store stress. You'll end up in a permanent knot. Instead, sample these ten strategies to reduce stress and promote mental health on the job.

Simple Pleasures

Most schools were not constructed with aesthetics in mind. Actually, there's little evidence of any thought beyond containment—institutional architecture at its finest. While corporate America toils in glass and marble towers, the CEOs of schools scramble for mismatched furniture to complement their World War II green walls. No surprise, working in an environment that looks like an institution makes one feel like—you guessed it—an inmate! So fight back. Stock your cell with simple pleasures that simulate all the senses. It's not *feng shui*, but I guarantee your mental state will shift noticeably toward the positive.

Music

Get it. Play it. All kinds. All day. With a modest music library, you can soothe or energize yourself at the touch of a button—or mouse. If there's a CD player in your computer, bring in your favorite CDs and strike up the band. Or get an inexpensive tape or CD machine, cue up your favorite artists, and your spirits will soar. With a stack of loud and lively disks, you can ratchet up your energy after hours and attack that mountain on your desk. With the right composer, it may even feel like fun.

Aromatherapy

Most offices smell like one of two things. Old carpet or new. Not attractive. So give your nose a break. Get sprays, potpourri, scented candles, or incense. Once your staff stops pouncing on the fire alarm every time you strike a match, everybody will settle down and enjoy the olfactory festival. Look for cedar, pine, and sage incense that capture the scent of the forest in autumn.

Eye Candy

I hate phones. Hate the way they make me jump. Their rude insistence during a quiet moment. The flurry of pink slips they generate with indecipherable messages—except for the word URGENT. I especially hate being tethered to my desk, on hold with bad music, or trapped on the receiving end of an angry but predictable monologue. So I keep a set of tiny photo albums nearby, crammed with New York street scenes or Toronto under snow. Instead of straining at the leash, I just flip through the photos and take a mental holiday. Dig out your favorite vacation or family photos, and give your eyes a treat. While you're at it, hang a few of your favorite posters, photographs, or paintings, too.

Passage to India

Here's the literary version of the photo album. Pile a half-dozen of your favorite books on your desk, with Post-it Notes on the best passages. When you need a lift, flip to a beloved paragraph. It's not like eating peanuts. You really will be able to stop. A little taste of literature goes a long way in the land of dreary memos.

Feed the Machine

Schools tend to be located in areas with high concentrations of children. By extension, that usually means a distinct absence of decent food outlets. So what's a starving administrator to do? Shuffle over to the cafeteria's carbohydrate buffet, or mug a small kid toting a packed lunch. There aren't many other options, which is why so many administrators act like survivors of the Donner Party at any meeting with refreshments. They're probably having their first meal of the day—at 4:00 P.M.

How do you avoid feeling like a famine victim in a business suit? Stockpile food. Trail mix, nuts, protein bars, peanut butter, juice, soy milk, protein powder, vitamins, and any sweets that your waistline and wardrobe will allow. Frequent snacks can sustain your energy and attitude throughout the longest day. Bon appetit!

Thoreau.com

Have you ever been in the heart of Manhattan at noon? Sneaker-clad people in chic business suits pour out of high-rises to grab a hot dog, a snootfull of taxi exhaust, and a walk. After a morning of cubicles and fluorescent light, they're finding refuge in the streets. You can, too. You don't need to be sequestered on Walden Pond to benefit from fifteen minutes of leg stretching. It's so little to give yourself considering the twelve-hour-plus days you're devoting to the school. You can take a speed-walk to jump-start your cardiovascular system, or saunter to search for signs of the season. Swing your arms, kick the leaves, breathe deeply. A daily walk can be a small but precious counterweight to the stress-laced atmosphere of your office.

> "A healthy and wholesome cheerfulness is not necessarily impossible to any occupation."
> —Mark Twain

Can't get out for a walk? How about a gym in your office? Not a treadmill—that would be redundant! I kept a set of dumbbells next to my phone and grabbed them throughout the day to make contact with my flagging triceps. No dumbbells? Hoist a heavy book. Do vertical push-ups. Stand about two feet from a wall, lean on it with straight arms, then ease yourself in and out. Sit in your chair, grab the seat, and lift your legs toward your chest to build leg muscles. If you've been hunched over your desk for hours, clasp your hands in a front of you, forming a circle with your arms. Lift your arms up and slightly behind your head. Stretch and repeat to relieve tension in your neck and shoulders. Stand up and do shallow knee bends. Any combination is great, since all progress is progress. The point is simply to give your muscles a quick romp throughout the day to prevent stress buildup and get much-needed oxygen to your brain.

There are also midget devices for shooting baskets or holes-in-one, plus many yoga stretches to relieve tension without ever taking off your jacket. Breathing is another powerful relaxation technique. Natural breathing is deep and slow. Under stress, we take little sniffs of air and return it to the atmosphere almost undigested. So switch your breathing from automatic to manual. While walking, inhale for five steps. Hold the air in for as long as comfortable, then exhale slowly for five steps. It's an effort at first, but well worth learning. Instead of snatching a tablespoon of air here and there, you force oxygen into your system. Your brain snaps to attention and your mood lifts.

Is This Hard?

Most of the work you do every day is important, but lots of it isn't hard. Before you get defensive and slam the book shut, think about it. How tough is it to have coffee and donuts with the carnival committee, supervise the cafeteria line, or oversee detention, for that matter? Yet many administrators are mainlining adrenaline all day long, even when moving from one relatively mundane task to another.

The problem is focus. They pile today, and this week, and the whole month on their shoulders, and then trudge through the daily grind. Now, that's hard. So here's a simple habit that breaks this stress cycle. As you start each activity, ask yourself: Is this hard? If the answer is no—relax. Be clear about your role, be alert, but most of all, consciously relax. Think of it as picnicking in the minefield.

I stumbled on this technique during an arduous IEP season. Parents routinely arrived with specialists, advocates, and assessment reports that would dwarf a phonebook. Three hours and seven experts later, we'd finish, quit, or reschedule, and then head for the next meeting. The toughest meetings were led by my talented colleague, Bill Himelright. One day, I looked across the table at him, and it just hit me like a brick. He was brilliant—so I could relax. The more I relaxed, the more effective I was with nervous parents and exhausted teams.

So get your finger off the adrenaline button. Put a Post-it with the question, Is this hard? on your daybook, phone, and computer. Just for practice, think of three activities from your day that aren't hard. Now make a habit of asking Is this hard? and give your frazzled nerves a rest.

Read All About It

My favorite principal, John Shambra, was a bookmonger. He never left his office without an intriguing title tucked under his arm. You needn't ask about his vision for the school—just trail him for a day. He was in and out of classrooms, reading aloud, determined to raise a crop of readers.

He knew the research—the greatest predictor that kids will become readers is if they are read to. He believed in the power of one—for some students he was the only adult in their lives who read for learning and pleasure. He insisted on having fun at his job every day, and reading to kids was his delight.

I've always read to my students—kindergarten through university—always with the same results. I glance up, five minutes into the story, and marvel at the utter repose of students lost in a book. Chins in hands, heads on tables, jaws slack with wonder. Then I relax, too.

> *"It is neither wealth nor splendor, but tranquility and occupation that gives happiness."*
> —Thomas Jefferson

Do your blood pressure a favor. Escape to classrooms and read aloud. For elementary students, my all-time favorite book is *Hey, Al* by Arthur Yorinks (1986), a tale of transformation and friendship. *The Giving Tree*, by Shel Silverstein (1964) is another great one, along with anything by Mem Fox. I'm sure you have your ten-best list.

Middle and high school students are just as easily mesmerized, probably because they're reliving a delight lost too soon. My father read to me and my four siblings until I was nearly a teenager, and it is one of my fondest childhood memories. So be brave. Read to older kids, but get the biggest bang for your buck by reading in their subject field. For example, when students study colonial history, read passages from *A Durable Fire* by Virginia Bernhard (1990), a magnificent novel about the first tragic years of Jamestown. Read slave journals to classes studying the Civil War. An amazing resource for titles is the website of the National Council of Social Studies. Go to the section on Notable Social Studies Trade Books, and browse extensive annotated bibligraphies for students of all ages. If you turn your teachers on to this site, you'll be vying for read-aloud time. Choose an artist's biography for studio classes. In a literature course, read your favorite poems. For composition students learning to write descriptive prose, read sections from *The Long Dark Tea-Time of the Soul* by Douglas Adams. Botany or geology students will appreciate sections of *A Walk in the Woods* by Bill Bryson.

The logistics are simple enough. John left a blank calendar of his reading times next to the teachers' sign-in sheet each Monday morning. It was full by noon. Try it. What could be better than a hour with your favorite book and a bunch of kids?

Enough Is Enough

As principal, you deal with the good, the bad, and the ugly. The good is you're the prime mover in hundreds or thousands of kids' education. That's hugely important. The bad—you're the prime mover in hundreds or thousands of kids' education. There's one of you, and legions of them. The ugly is that principals, as public servants, are increasingly subjected to abuse and threats from staff and community.

Timothy Dyer, deploring the suicide of a New York superintendent following an acrimonious board meeting, observed, "The thin veneer of civility within the educational community has been lost. Administrators have been required to accept in their public lives behavior which they would not tolerate in their private lives" (1997).

Your job description probably contains the phrase "and other duties as assigned," which may encompass ordering toilet paper or directing traffic, but it never includes verbal abuse or physical assault. Yet principals routinely encounter parents so explosive that they can clear a room. Not to mention the garden-variety drunks, bullies, and people with "Diminished Capacity" stamped on their foreheads. Even if you maintain the face of a Buddha and the composure of Ghandi, these clashes are megastressors.

I once had a brief but exciting appointment with a parent who looked like an itinerant electronics vendor, festooned with pager, tape recorder, and twin cell phones—lawyer on speed-dial, broker on hold. I had to admire his flair for technology, but what really got my attention was his unrelenting 300-megawatt grin, which he flashed while shoving a tape recorder in my face and shouting a string of abusive nonsequiturs, and which scarcely dimmed when he received a citation from the local police for using inappropriate language on school grounds.

Since it's impossible to eliminate these heart-stopping encounters, here are some techniques to use when bad behavior goes ballistic. Share these strategies with your staff at the beginning of every year, and review them periodically to enhance everyone's sense of security.

- Never respond to provocation. When the fight-or-flight instinct kicks in, the answer is *never* fight. Even if you have to shove your fist into your mouth up to your third knuckle, don't say what you're thinking. John Shambra's advice was, "Keep you hands in your pockets and say the fifth thing that comes to your mind."
- If tempers and volume escalate, or language takes a threatening turn, or even if the atmosphere just gets too tense or rude for your comfort level, end the meeting. In a calm voice, explain that you will be happy to reschedule, but, "Please understand. I don't feel we can have a productive meeting at this point."
- Stand up and walk toward the door or exit. Say, "I'm sorry that our meeting has to end this way. I truly hope that we'll be able to continue the conversation at another time." If the person refuses to leave the room, walk out anyway. That puts a stop to the encounter.
- Alert your staff to the problem, and ask someone to stay with you until the angry party departs.
- If the person tries to provoke you—"So you're calling my kid a liar"— or peppers you with questions to restart the conversation, use the broken record technique. Just repeat again in a calm voice, "I can't talk to you any more, but I hope we can continue on another day." It feels weirdly robotic, but you're winning by maintaining control.
- If the person refuses to leave or becomes more agitated, tell him or her that you will need to call campus security or the police. Then, follow through. Better safe than sorry. If the police arrive and write a report, get a copy.
- Document the entire incident in a short memo as soon as your hands stop shaking. Send it to the person at central office who handles legal matters, and inform your supervisor.
- If the behavior is repeated or escalates, the district can obtain a temporary restraining order (TRO) against the person, barring him from coming on campus without your express permission. This is a last resort and a real low point for school-family relations. If you are pushed to this point, make sure the student is insulated from the skirmishes and that your feelings toward the parent don't taint your relationship with the child.

After an encounter like this, get help. Debrief with your school psychologist, a counselor, or your therapist. Don't keep the trauma bottled up, where it can create a reluctance to meet with any parent. It's also good to go out and do something unusually nice for yourself. You always deserve it, but especially after shoddy or frightening treatment by a member of your school community.

Photo Safari

A school is a smorgasbord of lively images, and it doesn't take an Ansel Adams to see them. With a throw-away camera, novice documentarians can combine stress reduction with public relations. Taking pictures on campus forces you to focus—literally—on specific images within the swirling mass. Scanning for positive images reinforces what's good about your school and your job. Kids and teachers are flattered by your attention but curious about what you're seeing through that lens that's so special. They'll ask, giving you the perfect opportunity to share what you value in students and what's important work in classrooms.

With camera in hand, you can frame those "pictures of possibility" that constitute your vision, documenting the educational birthright in the flesh. And since a picture is worth a thousand words, these snapshots do double duty when you're talking to the community about this place called school. Have you ever met a parent who didn't pounce on any picture of his offspring? Me neither. So make your photos the first stop for the PTA crowd. Pin them to a rolling bulletin board, and drag it to every meeting you attend. It's another form of traveller's tales that visually reinforces your vision of how school and learning should look. Park the board in the front entry to greet visitors with a lively picture of kids and teachers at their best.

Roll your photo display into faculty meetings to reinforce what you value from your classroom observations. It's another way to say, "Bravo! Well done!" Teachers love to see their kids in the spotlight, and photo displays promote collegial conversations and collaboration. They highlight valuable ideas in a glance—creative teachers don't need much more to get their juices flowing.

I have a good 35mm camera but I'm just as fond of the disposable versions because I can slip them into my pocket. I keep a handful of mailers in my desk, so as soon as the roll is done, it's in the mail. If you have a digital camera, you can go wild. You can download and print your morning images for afternoon meetings, load them onto your website, email them to staff with Applause captions, and fire them off to board members, your mentor, or your supervisor. They will truly be worth a thousand words.

Applause, Applause

One of my mentor's favorite sayings was, "With all this manure, there has to be a pony around here somewhere." Ask any principal—kids are the ponies. You just have to find them. My suggestion is that you reserve part of each week for good kids, the ones who will never make it to your office on a referral—unless you retrain your staff. I had a delightful teacher, Diane Merz, who suggested this. She'd brief me on a student who deserved a pat on the back, then send him or her to my office. I'd chat with the surprised student a few minutes, and then came the surprise. We'd call the parents at home or work, and I'd say, "This is Laurel, the principal. Your child is in my office." Predictably, there was a gasp at this point—"because he has mastered his times tables. You must be very proud to have such a smart, hard-working son." After a minute, I'd put the student on the phone for more applause.

Some excellent students are just so much wallpaper at school, because they're quiet or self-effacing. As a result, they never experience the individual attention we lavish on more troubled students. But they need applause, too, and praise from the principal is high praise, indeed.

So try to see kids for good reasons. They can come to share their poems or journals, to discuss student council plans, or read aloud to you. These are some of the most authentic moments of the day, when you can be teacher, principal, and applause-machine all rolled into one

And while you're doling out all that applause, save a big helping for yourself. That's right. You need to be your own cheering squad, since there won't be many other applicants for the job. I created an Applause file and kept it in the top drawer of my file cabinet for easy access. Every time I got a note, card, or letter of encouragement, I'd tuck it in the file. The thicker it got, the better I felt. On days when I was down, I'd take a peek, and visualize those perky little yell leaders with pompoms and energy to burn, cheering for me. It's a simple way to document your impact and feel proud.

Houdini

There are times when you know you're on the brink of a spectacular burnout. An early morning plumbing disaster fertilized the locker room, student suspensions are breaking records, and faculty complaints are cheaper by the dozen. At two o'clock, you fortify yourself with a bag of chips and a warm coke. By three, you're staring down the barrel of a staff meeting, followed by a bracing round of paperwork, and a public free-for-all over the budget. Some people would be looking for a rope or a nice ledge-with-a-view. Instead, try a temporary escape. That's right. Escape. Disappear. Leave no forwarding address—without ever leaving campus.

Away.com

Tell your administrative assistant to hold your calls except for emergencies, with a capital *E*. Close your office door. Fire up the Internet and head straight for one of your favorite sites. To save time, bookmark at least a half dozen. If you love art, log on to a local museum for the latest exhibit, or visit the Metropolitan in New York. Hooked on history? Eavesdrop on those underwater archaeologists raising a Civil War sub. Motorcycle buff? Punch in Harley and drool over the latest models.

Maybe you love politics and global affairs. Click on the *New York Times*, the *Times of London*, the *Wall Street Journal*, or the *Washington Post*. Even if you just scan the headlines and scroll through a couple articles, you'll feel like you're part of the world beyond. And it's a great way to regain your perspective.

If Internet surfing seems too indulgent, log on to some leadership sites, or download the latest education legislation. The point is to vacate your life, and the Internet is your portal to the other side. Fifteen minutes in cyberspace and you'll be ready to face your world again.

Selected Internet Escapes

Leadership

www.clsr.org   Center for Leadership in School Reform

www.carfax.co.uk/slm-ad-htm   School Leadership and Management International

www.nsba.org/sbot/toolkit   Education Leadership Toolkit

www.nsba.org.cosa   Council of School Attorneys

www.ed.gov/pubs/leadership   Publications on Leadership

International News

www.onlinenewspapers.com   International News

www.library.uncg.edu/news   News and Newspapers Online

www.webwombat.com   Web Wombat

Museums

www.musee-online.org   MUSEE
www.museumca.org/usa   Oakland Museum of California
www.lib.washington.edu/sla/natmus.html   National History
Museums and Collections

History

www.historyplace.com   The History Place
www.thehistorynet.com   The History Net
www.hyperhistory.com   World History

Pasttimes

www.epicurious.com   Cooking
www.fromages.com   Cheese
www.sailnet.com   Sailing
www.hiking-tours-online.com   Hiking
www.pbaa.com   HikingCycling
www.skinet.com   Skiing
www.collectoronline.com   Antiques

Other Escapes

Use your computer to play a round of cards—solitaire or blackjack. If you don't have Internet access, or are cyberphobic, pick up the phone and call a really good friend, preferably a noneducator, so you can chat about everything but. If you get a machine, leave a detailed message. Even talking to a friend's voice mail feels better than nothing at all. Or paw through your Rolodex until you get a live one on the other end. Friends remind you of your value in the world and restore your perspective on a gloomy day. Make dinner plans. Pencil in a massage appointment or tee time. Consult your calendar for the next possible getaway dates, and call the airlines to check on fares. All of these activities lower stress because, despite the fact that you are locked in your office, they connect you to life beyond the job.

Clean Thoughts on a Dirty Wall

So many situations at school defy logic. Parking-lot rage over preferred spaces. The designated whiner at faculty meetings. The hue and cry over red-paper hoarding before Valentine's Day. At best, they test your patience. At worst, they make you want to bite. In lieu of sputtering, eye rolling, and slapping my forehead after such events, I would simply repeat, *All part of life's colorful pageant*, over and over, like a mantra, until I tricked myself into appreciating the humor of the situation. I swear—mantras work. If you don't have your own, borrow mine. They've seen me through some pretty tough times.

Mantras for Problem Solving

All progress is progress.

Everything should be made as simple as possible, but not simpler.

Imagination is more important than knowledge.

There are no rules here. We're trying to accomplish something.

A good plan today is better than a perfect plan tomorrow.

When you come to a fork in the road, take it.

You can't tell which way the train went by looking at the tracks.

Deliberate often—decide once.

The only way around is through.

Learn the rules so you know how to break them.

Freedom lies in being bold.

Mantras for Restoring Perspective

All things considered, I'd rather be in Philadelphia.

This is not the UN.

It is not a feat to travel the smooth road.

There's less to this than meets the eye.

When choosing between two evils, I always like to take the one I've never tried before.

There cannot be a crisis next week. My schedule is already full.

Diplomacy is the art of saying "nice doggy" until you find a rock.

When skunks duel, wind direction is everything.

We will burn that bridge when we come to it.

No good deed goes unpunished.

Mantras for Mental Health

Whatever doesn't kill me, strengthens me.

Harmony rarely makes headlines.

Too much of a good thing can be wonderful.

Misery is optional.

All part of life's colorful pageant.

Living well is the best revenge.

Or use lines from your favorite comedy routines. Taken out of context, they're emotional shorthand that no one else can read. I can't tell you how many times I've chuckled over, "Time is an illusion. Lunchtime doubly so," from *The Hitchhiker's Guide to the Galaxy* by Douglas Adams (1980). It doesn't matter that no one else understands. Mantras lift my spirits.

In the Moment

Stress is a nagging companion. It spoils perfectly good moments, usually by reminding you of something unpleasant in the past or the future. Your stress muscles hold on to little mistakes, and brace for big ones that might never come. The best way to fight those intrusions is to stay in the moment. Look at what you are doing well. Insist on having fun, even with simple tasks. Stop before you're exhausted. Go home early at least once a week. And remember, when you're lying on your deathbed, it's unlikely that you'll be thinking, "I wish I'd written one more memo."

15
Warpaint
Getting Smarter Under Fire

- Spot the Top-Ten Problems
- Manage Your Image
- Manage the Crisis
- Manage the Message

My mentor's favorite saying was "If they don't ask you to drink the hemlock, you're not doing the job." Some days that actually cheered me up. His gift was tricking me into feeling like I was doing something right, when everything felt so wrong. I wonder what he would have said to the principal who arrived at her faculty meeting ten minutes late and was greeted by staff members rhythmically pounding the tables and chanting "Where's the f—ing principal?"

If you've been a principal for any length of time, you've probably had your season in hell. That doesn't mean you're a bad principal. In fact, it may mean you're very good. But the job is rich with potential problems. Sometimes they start quietly and build to a painful crescendo, as with the principal who decided to enforce the discipline policy for all students, including upper-middle-class, white, honors students who were selling drugs on campus. Before long, he was denounced as ignorant, heavy-handed, and not a "good fit" for the community. Influential parents lobbied board members for his removal, as only campaign contributors can.

Some problems spring up like toadstools after a rain, blind-siding administrators like the ones who approved *Harry Potter* as an alternate literature choice, only to discover that they had "opened the floodgates for satanic influence."

It's nearly impossible to predict which events will trigger an explosion. That's why it's called the minefield. The job is tough. Principals who do it well are asking for trouble. The job is perilous.

Principals routinely work under fire with little district support, clinging to their professional lives. On any day they can awaken to the sickening realization that their career is circling the drain. Some are fired for blatantly political reasons or no discernible reason at all. It's the nature of life in the minefield.

What about you? Do you ever check your suit for bullet holes after community meetings? Or suppress the urge to install metal detectors on the doors of the faculty lounge? When you fire up your computer, do you hallucinate a cheery "You've got hate mail!" If so, drink up! You've got lots of company.

> *"Courage is not the absence of fear, but rather the judgement that something else is more important than fear."*
> —Ambrose Redmoon

School leadership is an exercise in crisis management because, as a principal, you routinely face issues for which you have not been trained, and for which there are no clear answers. The potential for mistake making is almost unlimited among novices and veterans alike. In any week, you may deal with vandalism, assaults, suicide threats, bomb threats, weapons, hostile parents, drunken students, disgruntled ex-employees, violent intruders, strikes, lawsuits, or hostage situations. There's no playbook for most of those events. So you rely on your wits and instinct. Sometimes that's not enough.

For every hundred things you do well, there's one decision that could lead to private humiliation or a public brawl. That's the nature of the job, and wanting it to be different is either a pipe dream born of fatigue, or a sign that you need to move on. But there are skills that experts use when they are facing a crisis.

When Trouble Calls: The Top-Ten List

First, let's take a look at the top-ten list of near-death experiences for administrators. If you wake up in the middle of the minefield, it's likely that you're dealing with one of these issues.

School Safety

In this post-Columbine, post–World Trade Center era, no one can sanely cling to the belief that, "it will never happen here." Nevertheless, proactive safety efforts are unglamrous and underfunded. But if there's a breach of security on your campus, or an accident at a school-sponsored event, you will be subject to intense scrutiny and could be the star witness in a host of lawsuits.

Discipline

Zero tolerance has wrought havoc with discipline procedures. Administrators are simultaneously attacked for their decisions by parents of the perpetrators and the victims. And don't forget the lawyers. The straw that recently broke a principal's back was hearing himself being mocked on a local radio-talk show for suspending a student.

Firing Employees

There are very few employees who can't raise a crowd of vocal supporters when firing is imminent. They question your decision, your ethics, your competence. They may even set up a legal fund for the teacher. Your supporters will be noticeably absent at times like this.

Special Education

Failing to address special needs, either IEPs or 504s, can lead to due-process hearings, inquiries from the Office of Civil Rights, complaints from the State Department of Education, class-action suits, or being verbally flayed during public comments at your board of education meetings.

Full Inclusion

Mainstreaming children with severe disabilities is a double-edged sword. Some parents push to keep their kids with disabilities in regular education settings, even if the team recommends a more restricted approach. Meanwhile, parents of kids with no disabilities object because the teacher has to spend so much time with special needs students. You may find yourself caught in the cross fire, both advocating for inclusion and filing for due process to gain a more restrictive placement, depending on the student.

Test Scores

Low test scores scores are one sure way to get your school in the local newspaper. And it's easier for parents to discuss your failure as a school leader, than to study disaggregated data about race, ethnicity, socioeconomic status, and underfunding. Test success can be tricky, too. A novice principal earned the wrath of veteran staff and the union when she credited the jump in test scores to the hard work of her new teachers.

Changing Curriculum

Changing curriculum can trigger a brawl if the haves feel that some of their advantage is being eroded by efforts to help the have-nots. A colleague of mine was driven out of her school when she disagreed with parents who felt their gifted kids should be segregated from the average-IQ bunch and given a multitude of expensive services to address their cognitive differences, sort of like their own private IDEA, but without the laws or funding.

Changing the School Day

The school day ranks right up there with the bald eagle as a protected species. So efforts to improve instruction through block scheduling, banking time, or split reading can bring a school administrator to his knees. Concern from parents is expected because they're juggling work, day care, and car pools. But your toughest opponents may be internal. As few as 20 percent of the teachers on a staff can block any restructuring effort. It feels like civil war and the collateral damage can be substantial.

Un-Sins

Being unreachable, unorganized, uninformed, unresponsive are sins of perception, which, via the grapevine, take on a reality that you may never shake. If you return fifty phone calls but receive seventy-five, you have huge exposure as an unresponsive leader. If people call and get a complete round of voice mail, you're dubbed the virtual administrator. If you fail to immediately inform the community of an incident on campus, you're negligent. Send home incorrect information—unacceptable. Eventually, you won't have enough support to survive.

Crossing Swords with Your Boss

When the political stakes are high, your relationship with your boss can go from cordial to refrigerated in the time it takes a dozen donuts to disappear from the faculty lounge. *Fired* is the ultimate f-word. Euphemisms such as "not a good fit" or "nonreelected" can't mask the humiliation. Being terminated strikes at the heart of who you are, and who you want to be. Job hunting, interviewing, and putting a good face on your departure under such a burden of failure can feel like scaling Everest without oxygen.

Dead Man Walking

When principals swap their top-ten horror stories, the conversations are more sporting event than therapy because the my-scar-is-bigger-than-yours impulse usually gets in the way. Sometimes their injuries are disguised by bravado, but under the toughened exterior, nerve endings still twitch at the mention of collective bargaining. Others have visible wounds that are freshened at every governance meeting or town hall gathering.

Whether they call it a minefield or just say the job is a daily challenge, most principals will readily admit that their work has an explosive potential that makes Krakatoa look like a theme-park attraction. Day after day, they gather their professional resources and wade into the fray, armed with statements like, "We have a vibrant community and a challenging situation. But with vigorous public interest and strong staff input, I believe we can construct a compelling dialogue between diverse groups to address these important of issues." Translation: "Running interference between staff, community, and the district feels like the agony trifecta."

One way principals survive the toughest times is to adopt the Dead Man Walking approach. It comes in several unfortunate versions. One is to induce a state of professional numbness—fight but never feel the blows. Another approach is to find a safe patch of ground and freeze, since doing nothing prevents further exposure. More common is the attempt to please everyone and offend no one, which inevitably backfires and pleases no one. A few school leaders use a stalking-horse—like an assistant principal—to test the ground, take the hits, and report back, so the unsullied principal can tread a safe path. All of these strategies have a high personal price because they only work if part of you dies—or at least achieves a persistent vegetative state. Dead emotions, dead vigor, dead ethics. Plus, you risk looking ineffective, two-faced, cowardly, or insensitive. So what's the alternative?

Preparation, courage—and pain.

You won't know what form your crisis will take until you're in the middle of it. It could be a conflict of your own making, like mine. I decided to truly observe and evaluate teachers, in defiance of the local tradition, and landed a spot on the union's most-wanted list for several years running. Then there's the principal who will spend the last years of his career responding to interrogatives from a small platoon of lawyers because a private swimming party to celebrate fifth-grade graduation went horribly wrong—a child nearly drowned. The invitations were passed out at school, the whole class was invited, and thus, the school is forever linked to the tragedy.

Whether your predicament is over personnel, policy, or politics, there are skills that can help you manage the crisis itself, and the message that the community hears. But first and foremost, you must be able to manage your own image. Perception is paramount when a crisis hits.

Manage Your Image

When you're under pressure or under fire, people tune in as if it were *Days of Our Lives*. Your supporters are checking, sometimes hourly, to see if you're still standing. They need you to look strong so that they can feel safe. The loyal opposition is just as vigilant, measuring the impact of their latest assault. It is critical that you look secure and successful, even if you feel like you're on death row. For a start, you'll need to show up every day—that alone takes energy and courage. But it's no good to limp in, looking like the loser in a ten-round brawl. No matter how lousy you feel, you need to wear warpaint! Here are six techniques that nonverbally communicate an image of confidence and competence, at the best of times, and especially at the worst.

Posture

Concentrate on your posture. Good posture sends a message of confidence and energy. It signals relaxation. More important, you feel different when you stand erect. Slumping and slouching make you look and feel weary, deflated, and weak.

Gestures

Change your gestures. People who know you recognize your nervous habits. They know that you adjust your glasses, lick your lips, tap your fingers, smooth your clothes, adjust your watch, pace, or stutter when you're working at the outside limits of your knowledge or courage. So concentrate on changing your gestures. If you usually punctuate your sentences with your hands, rest them in your lap. If you're a foot jiggler, plant your feet on the floor and keep them there. Delete stock phrases like "But in the same sense . . ." that make you sound like you're equivocating.

Facial Expressions

If anxiety becomes the central feature of your life, you may unconsciously freeze your face in a neutral expression to mask your emotions, or exaggerate your expressions, plastering on a 500-watt smile when you would rather bite. If your words and facial expressions are at odds, people notice. So monitor your expressions and work on relaxing your facial muscles. Smile. Greet everyone you pass on campus. Never mumble, pout, or look angry.

> *"Eighty percent of success is showing up."*
> —Woody Allen

Personal Appearance

When I was crisis-ridden, I would routinely awake at 4:23 A.M. with a stomachache that I could sell to science. My face told the story in the morning. So if you're not sleeping, spend extra time on your appearance. Choose a new image—more casual to show confidence, more formal to show power. Wear outfits that become you. Get a new hairstyle, bigger jewelry, brighter ties. Change the frame of your glasses, grow a beard, wear aftershave. Personal renovation is the sign of a winner.

Eye Contact

Eye contact is a sign of interest. Failing to connect conveys disinterest, distance, arrogance, or preoccupation. It can also signal discomfort or guilt. You might avoid making eye contact for fear that a single glance will reveal feelings, like anger or fear, that you would rather hide. A steady gaze helps you look in control.

Proximity

The distance you set between yourself and others can send strong messages of interest or avoidance. Standing too close can feel threatening—too far, people feel like they haven't captured your attention. Your desk can seem like a barricade or signal authority. Sit behind it if you need to add power or sternness to your usual approach. Come out and sit facing a person to communicate respect and interest.

An Exercise

You can use your physiology to trick yourself into feeling relaxed, confident, and in control. Try this. Smile. Stand tall, arch your shoulders back, slap a great big smile on your face and stride briskly around your office or around the block. Grin. Beam. Twinkle. Your body will trick your brain into elevating your mood. That's right. Your brain is conditioned to think that a smile means you are happy, so it looks for reasons to justify the physical signal you're sending. You may experience a flood of positive memories as your brain finds a match for your tooth display. Other people around you may smile, reinforcing your sense of well-being. At the very least, you will send a message to everyone who sees you that you are happy. People want that in a leader. It makes you look secure and promotes mental health in the organization.

Manage the Crisis

Crises come in all flavors. Principals have found themselves staring down the barrel of a gun, then, minutes later, down the barrel of a CNN microphone—with no warning and no script. Politics and pedagogy swirl around them all the time, and occasionally they're swept into the vortex. You may go to battle against your community with every teacher standing behind you or find yourself in a battalion of one. When controversy surrounds you, use some or all of these strategies to manage the crisis.

Do Your Homework

Gather data. Read. Research similar situations on the Internet. Contact your professional association for position papers, pending legislation, exemplary programs or training, including crisis management skills.

Call in the Experts

Principals under fire are sometimes reluctant to call for help in the early stages of a problem, but more often they're just too busy minding the store, so by the time they call in reinforcements, the situation has gone from smoke to inferno. Train yourself. At the first quease of your stomach or whiff of smoke, start dialing for support. Call peers, central office staff, the County Office of Education, the State Department of Education, the district lawyer, your professional organization's lawyer, the district's communications or public information officer, and of course, your mentor. If your situation is critical, call the person with the most knowledge or clout first. Don't get caught in negative self-talk, like *I should know how to handle this, maybe I made a mistake, what will people think?* They'll think you're smart if you ask for help.

Issue Invitations

When you're in the midst of a crisis, instinct will tell you to close your office door and take the phone off the hook, or go after someone with a cudgel. Override instinct. Keep the door open for problem solving. When informed that the staff feels harassed by your evaluation techniques or disagrees with your plan for tardy sweeps, say, "Thank you for that information. I'd appreciate it if you would write me a note to that effect, so I can follow up. Let's meet to talk about it. Who else should we include?" If two people show up, it's a safe bet that "the staff" has little investment in the issue. I've prepped for meetings in auditoriums because a hundred people were expected, and found myself making small talk with nineteen sheepish adults and seventy-nine folding chairs.

When meeting with adversaries or warring factions, agree on a goal, set a time line, and insist on a product. Publish the minutes of the meeting and invite interested parties to the next. In other words, turn the problem into a project. Work it through face-to-face, systematically, rather than staging skirmishes or retreating into isolation. If the will to work is there, you can be on your way to a solution or at least a neutral workplace.

Beef Up the Broadcasts

Your opponents in any conflict usually have one big advantage—free time. While you're holding down the fort, they're cranking out bulletins on their point of view. Fight back. Flood the airwaves with the positive side of the story, but not just from your lips. Publish data, research, legislation, ideas from award-winning schools, expert points of view. Educating your community on the finer points of a controversy is the most effective way to enlarge the conversation. People who have facts are less susceptible to rumors.

Weigh Your Words

When handling a crisis, you need to be on full alert every time you open your mouth. But realistically, this is a time when you will have the least stamina, the lowest frustration tolerance, the highest level of provocation, and the greatest urge to shoot from the lip. Do not do it.

If you are at odds with staff or community, many things will be said about you that will be inaccurate or utterly false. That is especially so in wired communities, where the rumor mill is a high-tech, wholesale, dot-com enterprise. The listserver is not your friend. You may receive disturbing emails penned by a foe or forwarded by a friend. Resist the urge to have an online debate. The forward button means that your remarks, edited or otherwise, can be sent out to hundreds of people without your permission or knowledge.

Unwitnessed Acts

During a crisis or dispute, people will ask for private meetings with you. Two people will ask for an appointment—a delegation from the UN will show up. At least one person will be taking notes. If anyone pulls out a yellow legal tablet, you may have a lawyer in the group, preparing a brief for court. Ask the note taker to identify herself, and always ask if there are any lawyers in the group. If so, you're on thin ice. End the meeting until a district lawyer can be present. Always have someone else in the room taking notes. Take notes yourself. Date and sign them. Xerox copies and add them to your file.

Cochair

During a crisis, never assume that an invitation to address a group or to drop by a community meeting is a neutral event. I know an administrator who did, and left with the label racist and a fresh crop of bruises. Don't do difficult meetings alone. Get a district official whose job is most closely related to the fracas to come out and cochair the meeting. He can answer the technical questions, or just take the heat while your collect your wits. Having a partner helps you do a better job of getting your story out.

Document

Documenting is one of the hardest things to do in a crisis, and one of the most important. You need to create a record of what you did and didn't do and say. But during a crisis you have less than no time. Every moment you spend in damage control, communication, or consultation puts you further behind in your regular work. So documenting is just another task that you don't have time to do. But it can save you lots of agony if this issue hits the press, mediation, or a lawsuit.

Your memory won't serve you. So document every phone call, meeting, decision, and directive to staff. Start a file and throw in anything of relevance including copies of emails, downloads of relevant material from websites, citations from the *Education Code*, phone logs, Xeroxed notes to teachers, meeting agendas, school rules, newsletters, or staff bulletins. If you have a trusted assistant principal, debrief with that person each day. Review events, make notes, and strategize.

Manage the Message

There was once a school fight that made the five o'clock news despite the principal's effort to quell the coverage. Or rather, because of it. Twenty to thirty high school students had a lunchtime clash, and thanks to cell phones, camera-toting reporters materialized while a dozen arms and legs were still flying. Over the shouts of students and questions of reporters, the principal insisted, "I have nothing to tell you" and clamped his hand over the lens of the camera, looking like a mobster who'd just made bail. Not his finest hour! With a bit of coaching, he could have sent a message about school safety that would have reassured the community and built confidence in his leadership skills. Read all about it.

Feed the Machine

If the media decides that your grief is film-at-eleven, you'll need to be prepared. In some crises, the police, the superintendent, or the district public information officer may handle the press. But if you are on your own, or you are expected to speak at some point, it's important that you understand the role of the press. The first thing to realize is that your needs and the needs of the media are compatible in a crisis. At first glance this may seem insane. No one wants to train a spotlight on their campus when things have gone very wrong, especially if you're the person in charge. Yet talking to the media helps you get accurate information out to the community, and let's you control and represent the story.

Keep this phrase in mind—*Feed the machine*—and everything else falls into place. Most reporters are good people who want to do their job. They will get their story with or without you, precisely because it's their job. Television reporters covering a sensational story such as Columbine need on-camera updates every twenty minutes. So you can talk to them, or they'll find a student, parent, or staff member, and report whatever they can cobble together—even if it's inaccurate—just to feed the machine. Print reporters have the same motivation. They need to fill the white space, then they can go home. All of them want pictures.

So orchestrate media coverage. Designate a specific place for the press. Set a time for a minipress conference. If at all possible, set up a podium. Prepare a statement—one or two points that you want your audience—community, parents, board members, staff—to know. Working from notes is the best way to control the quotes. Then keep in mind that it's not an interview—it's an opportunity to get your story out to your constituents.

Always be truthful. A lie will kill you later. If you don't know the answer to a question, don't say "I don't know." Say, "I'll find out." If the crisis goes on for hours, you'll need a steady supply of information. Be prepared to supply data such as the size of your school, the number of students, the demographics, the performance level of the school, the history of violence, incidents on the campus, the administrative team. Dole this information out in small helpings at regular intervals along with updates. At the end of each press conference, tell reporters what time you will return, and be sure to do so.

If you are interviewed on camera, look at the reporter, not the camera. Don't shift your eyes back and forth. Don't leave your message behind. No matter what the question, return to your message. Don't lose your focus, even if the questions seem antagonistic or insensitive. A school tragedy is always a community tragedy. Frame your comments with "Our community . . ." Express concern for students and their families. Always praise the performance of your staff and their continuing focus on the welfare of their students.

Expect Tough Questions

Principals are question-magnets. They are peppered with interrogatives at PTA meetings, school tours, new-parent orientation, staff meetings, governance meetings, and of course, in the express checkout line of the supermarket. One Saturday morning I was cruising through the farmer's market, arugula in one hand and cantaloupe in the other, when a child screeched to a halt in front of me and joyfully announced, "It's Mrs. Principal." What followed was not so joyful—a fifteen-minute harangue by his mother about how he was developing school phobia because his teacher was so mean and why won't I move him to another class? There I stood in jeans and a sweatshirt, working on spin diplomacy and calculating how many minutes were left on my parking meter.

> *"Education is the ability to listen to almost anything without losing your temper or your self-confidence."*
>
> —Robert Frost

All of which is to say that the old social boundaries have

eroded significantly. People not only ask questions almost anywhere, anytime, but they also initiate probes so rude, accusatory, or downright dishonest that they make the Salem witch trials look like a conflict resolution seminar.

Avoid Verbal Land Mines

"Why are your test scores still so low?" is a question at least half the principals in the country dread. Or: "What are you doing about the violence on your campus?" "Why aren't there more minority kids in AP classes?" "Why can't you get qualified teachers to come to this school?" "When are you going to offer real science classes?" People who ask these questions are like ventriloquists. They know the answer they want. And they have the skills to make their words come out of your mouth. If you understand the game, you can turn their questions into a platform on which you perform brilliantly. By the time you get through, no one will even remember their needling remarks.

Here's how it's done. There are seven techniques that reporters, parents, staff, and community members use to tilt an interview in a negative direction and trap you into making statements that provide provocative sound bites or headlines. You need to study these ploys, learn to recognize them on the fly, and practice deflecting them intelligently. Your career may depend on it. They are:

1. The False Premise
2. Negative Entrapment
3. The Quotation
4. The Hypothetical Question
5. The Wedge
6. Unacceptable Choices
7. The Loaded Preface

Just tune in to any political talk show or Sunday morning news program for a primer in constructing and answering explosive questions.

The False Premise. Building a false or misleading assumption into a question forces you into a misleading response: "So are children really safe on buses without seatbelts?"

Negative Entrapment. The attempt to get you to say something negative results in an unflattering or unintended quote: "As a principal you must get awfully frustrated with a district that can't get its fiscal priorities straight from one year to the next and keeps slashing your budget. Is that the biggest challenge you face?"

The Quotation. The attempt to get you to respond to something someone may or may not have said results in a defensive and unflattering tone: "Amy Crispin says that you are unfairly stacking your hiring committees with minorities. What's your response to that?"

The Hypothetical Question. Hypothetical questioning traps you into an inconsistency by getting you to say one thing in a personal hypothetical situation and then contrasting it later to your reaction to a real situation: "If your child were at the same school as a student who created a website threatening to kill Persian students, wouldn't you think you had a right to know about it?"

The Wedge. Wedge questioning attempts to separate your opinion from that of someone with whom you should be aligned. If they can do that, the potential exists for a great conflict story and personal or professional trouble for you. "As principal you have to support a retention policy that you didn't even have a part in developing. A lot of researchers say that retention is never beneficial for students. Do you really support this policy?"

Unacceptable Choices. Some questions attempt to make you choose between two bad options, neither of which you should feel compelled to choose. "Your suspension rate for drug violations has skyrocketed. Is that because more drugs are being sold on your campus or you weren't enforcing district policy in the past?"

The Loaded Preface. Questions that include a whole laundry list of negatives before they get to the point are loaded. Your impulse will be to respond to each charge on the list. Counter instead by using it as an opportunity to say something good about your school. "There is this perception in the community that your school is the worst in the district. It has low test scores, gangs, drug-sniffing dogs. The police are on campus more often than some of your students and teacher absenteeism is scandalous. Why can't you do anything about these problems?"

> " *A smooth sea never made a skilled mariner.* "
> —English Proverb

The ABCs of a Successful Response

The first time you're slapped with a loaded question in public, it takes your breath away. Fielding a barrage of these zingers before a hostile crowd or a bevy of cameramen feels like being a product-tester for an electroshock company. But people who are on the firing line for a living, like public information officers, rely on a formula that converts loaded questions into public relations opportunities. It's as simple as ABC, which is good because when you're under fire, you can't think your way through every volley.

Study this formula, then turn on the Sunday morning political round-ups such as *Meet the Press* or *Face the Nation* to see it in action. Seasoned politicians, government spokespersons, and corporate representatives use the ABCs all the time to get their message out. Learn this technique. Practice in front of the mirror. It could save your life when you're in front of crowds or cameras. Here it is.

A—Acknowledge the question or statement.

B—Bridge to your prepared statement by telling the audience what you want them to know.

C—Convert the question to the message you want to send.

Here's how this would look.

Q: As a principal you must get awfully frustrated with parents who aren't involved with their children's education or who are bad role models for their children. Is that the biggest challenge you face?

A: Every position carries its rewards and challenges,

B: . . . but here at Cambridge Middle School,

C: . . . parent participation has grown steadily over the past three years and we expect that to continue thanks to our Parent Outreach Project, which offers parenting classes in our new community center, a video lending library, a broad range of volunteer opportunities, and ESL classes during the day and at night.

Here's another example.

Q: Your suspension rate for drug violations has skyrocketed. Is that because more drugs are being sold on your campus?

A: "We fully expected our suspension rate to increase in the first months of this school year; . . .

B: however, not for the reason you suggested.

C: In September, we implemented a zero-tolerance policy for drug possession, and I am happy to report that the incidence of possession this month has dropped to a single supension. We believe students now understand that we are very serious about helping them succeed in school and avoid substance abuse by having a drug-free campus.

> *"Difficulties strengthen the mind, as labor does the body."*
>
> —Seneca

Kindred Spirits in the Minefield

Surviving under fire is a daily struggle. Honing your skills will help, but some nights you'll need a strong shot of inspiration to keep you from throwing in the towel. I get mine from survivor autobiographies—where real leaders snatch themselves from the jaws of disaster. Books like *Personal History* by Katharine Graham (1997) or Martin Luther King Jr.'s *Stride Toward Freedom* (1986), about the Montgomery bus boycott, have taught me more about strategizing and raw courage than any of the "vision" books I've been forced to read. I love books about Elizabeth the First and Eleanor Roosevelt. I watched *Wag the Dog* more times than I care to admit, simply to condition my nerve endings to the notion that a crisis is an opportunity for creativity—and sometimes greatness.

16
Moving On
Getting Smarter About Time and Tide

- Location, Location, Location
- Moving On Up
- Back to the Classroom
- The Business of Education
- The Not-for-Profit World
- Author! Author!
- Retooling

All principals have days where they shake their heads and muse, "There's got to be more to life than this." Indeed, there are times when leading a school can feel like rearranging the deck chairs on the *Titanic*. But most principals also experience deep satisfaction on the job—usually from counseling students or mentoring teachers. That's what keeps them coming back day after day to the difficult, awesome challenge of being a principal, where rewards are measured in the self-confidence of a child, the triumph of students who truly learn how to learn, and the pride of teachers who have given their best.

The profession needs dedicated administrators. It needs you, for as long as you can provide the strong and stable leadership that is an essential ingredient of high-performing learning communities. Some principals last for decades, and become legends in their own time. Others use their experience as a foundation for central office leadership. Some retire, and turn their prodigious skills into interesting second or third careers. In a few cases, administrators discover that the job is simply not a good fit, and rather than lose their passion for education, they move on or return to the classroom.

If you're a principal considering a career change for any reason, you may be hampered by a narrow view of what's out there. Take heart! There's a vast array of opportunities waiting for you. You'll need to do some basic research and dust off your resume, but first and foremost, you need to be clear about what you want.

The solution may be as close as your own office, or as remote as a primary school in Pretoria. Finding the answer is an adventure in itself!

What Do You Really Want?

Thinking about a career change is a huge step—potentially so overwhelming that you might give up before you ever get to the resume-interview-I-love-my-new-job part. So think of this as a research project, with lots of little parts that you can do in your spare time. Start slowly. Make a file, go online, and keep notes. Most important, poke around inside your head to identify the good, the bad, and the tolerable about your current job. Some people make lists of pros and cons to get clarity. I like questions. Try these.

The Moving-On Questionnaire

Do I still feel passionate about this job?

How often do I feel satisfied at the end of the day?

What special skills do I have that are untapped in this setting?

Is there a different audience that I want to address?

What do I love about my current job?

What do I hate about this job?

Do I feel like I'm going through the motions?

Am I making a difference?

Can I do this work and still be myself?

Is my family paying too high a price for my career?

Is my physical health suffering?

Is my intellectual life on hold?

Am I ignoring my mental health, or does it take industrial-strength therapy to keep me sane?

If I could change one thing about my current job, what would it be?

If I accomplished that change, would I want to stay?

If I were paid more, would I stay?

What does my head say?

What does my heart say?

Do I have another dream?

What is my fantasy of a perfect job?

Be as truthful and specific as possible, because your answers hold valuable clues for making your current job more satisfying or preparing to move on. Armed with this information, you're ready to start crafting a plan to clarify your goals and investigate career improvement strategies.

Location, Location, Location

Maybe you still like many aspects of being principal, but just need a change of venue. Rethinking your location is a great way to improve your outlook and stay in a profession that truly needs talented, experienced leaders. Start with a math lesson. Take a minute to calculate the number of hours you spend commuting each week. If it's more than ten, imagine how you could use that time to improve your lifestyle. If it's approaching twenty, you're working half-time as a commuter. Look for a job closer to home.

Thinking that the grass is always greener can lead to a successful school change. You could find administrative nirvana and add years to your career simply by moving to a school that is smaller; a different level; more compatible with your vision; less pedagogically challenged; in a neighborhood that really needs you; or a magnet school with a focus such as science, humanities, or the fine arts, that matches your area of expertise.

> "When one door closes, another door opens; but we often look so long and so regretfully upon the closed door that we do not see the ones that open for us."
>
> —Alexander Graham Bell

Perhaps it's not the school itself, but the administrative landscape that's become barren, convoluted, or fraught with political strife. In changing districts you may gain new colleagues among whom you can find support, a new superintendent with a different leadership style, or a coprincipalship so you won't have to go it alone.

Another option is to do some sampling before you relocate. New York City started the millenium with two hundred administrative vacancies. There are empty slots all over the country—the larger the district, the greater the need. So there's a whole new rent-a-principal market that may provide a very appealing change of pace. You work on a per diem basis in a temporary assignment, so you don't know or owe anyone. That gives you a free hand or, at the very least, a sense of detachment that keeps your stress level down. Who knows? If it's a good fit, you may have a new place to call home.

Independent Schools

If you've spent most of your career in public education, struggling with crumbling facilities, underfunding, overregulation, and the labyrinth of the public process, you may not realize that there's a parallel universe where educational philosophy, best practices, academic rigor, and meeting individual student needs are the rule of the day and where teachers demonstrate high professional standards or find a new job at the end of the year.

Independent schools are private, nonprofit schools governed by boards of trustees and supported by tuition, private gifts, grants, and endowments. They range in size from several dozen to thousands of students. Their approaches to teaching cover the spectrum from team-taught classes, project-centered curriculums, and experiential classes to industrial-strength academics. They can be a haven for passionate administrators who yearn to put their stamp on an educational enterprise. They're not perfect. The demands of fund-raising and local politics require long hours and excellent public relations skills. But they may be a perfect fit for you.

A quick tour of independent school sites on the Internet turned up several jobs, fully loaded with administrative accessories. For a start:

> Immediate opening for a Headmaster of a Pre-K through 8th grade nonsectarian independent school for gifted and talented students. 150 students, 32 staff members. To learn more about the school, visit the website.

I did, and drooled on my keyboard. Another advertisement seeks:

> Director of Admissions and Financial Aid to represent the school in the broader community, be an enterprising recruiter, write and speak with clarity, and have a desire to become an integral member of an exciting school community.

Did I mention the forty acres of land and a four-million-dollar endowment for 325 students? If this sounds intriguing to you, go online to begin your investigation, stopping off at these sites.

National Association of Independent Schools   www.nais.org

Independent Schools Association of the Southwest   www.isasw.org

Independent Schools Association of the Cental States
www.isacs.org

Pacific Northwest Association of Independent School
www.pnais.org

Southern Association of Independent Schools   www.sais.org

National Association of Private Schools for Exceptional Children
www.napsec.com

Canadian Association of Independent Schools   www.cais.ca

Conference of Independent Schools (Canada)   www.cis.edu.on.ca

Globe-Trotting

Picture an office overlooking a colorful street market in Singapore or nestled in a seventeenth-century villa in Florence. Imagine trying to finish a teachers' bulletin, distracted by the sunset over the Pyrenees, or a sudden snowfall in Paris. It could happen to you, because there's a farflung network of international schools that serve English-speaking students around the world. Every year they host bustling job fairs to lure experienced administrators with hefty salaries, generous moving allowances, and return tickets at the holidays. The Internet is a perfect tool for exploring these daydreams or making them a reality. A brief visit to a single site revealed the following opportunities:

> *"Life was meant to be lived and curiosity be kept alive. One must never, for whatever reason, turn his back on life."*
>
> —Eleanor Roosevelt

- Superintendent (Lima, Peru)
- Director (Aberdeen, Scotland)
- Headmaster (Santiago, Chile)
- Superintendent (San Pedro Sula, Honduras)
- Director (Warsaw, Poland)

Start with International Schools Services Service (www.iss.edu) online for a detailed description of their recruitment service, frequently asked questions about working abroad, setting up a professional file, and time lines for selecting candidates. Then track down any of the following organizations online for lists of more openings and application procedures.

The Principal's Training Center for International School
http://members.aol.com/theptc

Office of Overseas Schools in the U. S. Department of State
www.state.gov/m/a/os

Overseas Schools Assistance Corporation   www.tieonline.com

European Council of International Schools   www.ecis.org

Mediterranean Association of International Schools
www.mais.org

Association of American Schools in South America
www.aassa.com

East Asia Regional Council of Overseas Schools   www.earcos.org

Near East South Asia Council of Overseas Schools
www.nesacenter.org

After the initial thrill of country shopping wears off, you may want some practical information. A cottage industry exists just to help people like yourself expatriate. Try any of these sites.

www.ReloGlobal.com	Currency converters, taxes, time zones
www.EscapeArtis.comt	Country and regional guides, newspapers
www.ExpatAccess.com	Practical tools and assistance for locating internationally
www.ExpatForum.com	Information about living, working, and traveling abroad
www.iteachnet.com	International Teachers Network. Information about schools from people who have worked there.

Moving On Up

Surviving a principalship is great training for almost any job in the central office. After all, you've seen it all from the other side—while dodging the bullets. Most central-office jobs require administrative experience, but rarely the nerves of steel or body armor you need at a school site. So if you like your district team, you may love the relative calm of a central-office position. Examine your personal strengths, assess your transferable skills, and consider any of the following jobs as a logical next step.

Human Resources

Human resources presents a perfect example of transferable skills. As a principal, you know how to recruit, screen, interview, hire, supervise, coach, evaluate, and fire everyone from a health-office clerk to a coadministrator. You've committed large parts of the contract to memory, and been up close and personal with the bargaining unit more times than you care to remember. Just throw in a credential technician and some job fairs, and you're on your way to happiness in human resources.

Pupil Services

Pupil services is an interesting job, part legal, part child welfare, part public relations. If you like policy, research, discipline, school safety, attendance, student advocacy, counseling families, and problem solving in a format that changes every day, look into this. You'll still get your share of cranky parent calls, but they won't be mad at you.

Director of Grants Development

Many districts make the leap from ordinary to distinguished through generous and prestigious grants that provide multiyear funding for innovative programs. If you have strong communication skills, a good grip on current educational directions, a taste for data and research, and a curiosity about other agencies, this could be a great fit for you. Some districts have entire departments, others just a lone grant writer with a high tolerance for deadlines. Check it out.

Curriculum and Instruction

This seems like a no-brainer. Even the smallest district has someone minding the learning store. Curriculum and instruction jobs will include any or all of the following responsibilities: develop improvement strategies; plan, organize, and design curriculum, and instruction for second-language learners and gifted students; organize assessment; plan and deliver staff development, evaluate textbooks and other learning materials. It's a huge, interesting job, especially if you're fascinated with how kids and adults learn.

Public Information Office

Public information jobs are not everyone's cup of tea, but if you were blessed with a silver tongue and titanium nerves, this could be right for you. Your intimate knowledge of how schools work could give you a leg up over other PIOs who may have come from the communications field. You'll be working behind the scenes writing press releases, designing websites, creating brochures, collaborating with grant writers and recruiters. You'll be out front during a crisis, dealing with the media or feeding lines to the people who meet the press.

Life at the Top

For those of you who long to see the view from the top of the organization chart, even for a few battle-scarred years, investigate life as an assistant super-intendent, superintendent, or director at your county office of education. Your local, state, or national leadership journal is thick with advertisements for superintendents. Just be sure to research the potential position thoroughly. Online local newspapers are your first best source of information about the community, the board, and why the last superintendent left. Then hook up with experts who know the specific challenges presented by board politics, student achievement levels, and labor issues before you commit yourself to the big leap.

Back to the Classroom

Some of my happiest hours as a principal were spent teaching kids. I loved stepping in when a substitute was late, or taking over the mentor's class so she could work with a novice teacher. Some days, my nostalgia for the classroom ached like a phantom limb. I know I wasn't alone in feeling that, as principal, I was missing out on the best part of the whole enterprise.

So one of your options is to find yourself a teaching gig. The most obvious is to return to your old job, but this can be psychologically difficult, especially if principals in your district enjoy high status and stepping down is perceived as failure. On the other hand, it may be the most sane and liberating move you'll ever make.

There are other opportunities that can get you back to the chalkboard. Consider teaching your peers. All over the continent, there are organizations dedicated to raising a new crop of administrators and supporting the troops in the field. Investigate staff positions at principal's centers, leadership institutes, university programs, or in districts that have formed their own administrative farm teams.

If your strength is in curriculum and instructional strategies, hook up with the local colleges or universities that have credential programs. Most of these institutions hire adjunct professors to teach one or more courses. Junior colleges are another possibility, since many have child development programs for child-care workers and parents. For information on college positions, check these organizations as a starting point:

Higher-Education Jobs www.higheredjobs.com
Academic Position Network www.apnjobs.com
Affirmative Action Register www.aar-eeo.com

Academic 360.com   www.academic360.com

American Association of Colleges for Teacher Education
www.aacte.org

American Education Research Association   www.AERA.net

The Business of Education

Administrators longing for a complete career change may lose heart, mistakenly seeing themselves as one-trick ponies. *All I've ever done is teach. Is the classroom my only option?* But many jobs in the for-profit world rely on people with the exact skill set that you've been perfecting for years. Look at it this way. You mastered multitasking before it had a name. You handle a thousand human interactions a day, most requiring educational expertise, diplomacy, and split-second decisions. What business wouldn't benefit from a few more people like you?

Publishers

Educational publishing is a billion-dollar industry that depends on a steady supply of writers, editors, trainers, and consultants. These companies hire armies of freelance employees who are paid very well compared to the in-house staff. The more you know about curriculum and best practices, the greater the possibilities for employment. Start your inquiries with any of the publishers who specialize in textbooks. A tour of the book room at your school will give you a short list, and as always, the Internet is a trove of information on publishers.

There is also a broad range of educational publishing aside from the business of textbooks. These publishers need freelance and staff writers, editors, and representatives with an understanding of education. You've been in the driver's seat, so you have a lot to offer. Check the AcqWeb Directory online for names and locations of companies in educational publishing.

Training, Workshops, and Speakers Bureaus

Like many other public enterprises, education supports a vast constellation of private companies in the business of helping teachers and administrators get better at what they do. To locate these companies, just monitor the junk mail that arrives at your front office each week. All those colorful flyers for conferences, seminars, workshops, professional development courses, training sessions, and speakers were sent by potential employers.

Just pick up the phone, dial the 800 number, and ask to talk to the professional development director. If that doesn't work, ask for the recruiter or simply say that you're interested in being a trainer or presenter for their organization.

Companies that hire presenters for educational seminars have an application process that requires you to submit some combination of the following: an outline for the seminar you want to teach, your resume, a list of seminars you have conducted for adults, the names of five or six individuals who have seen you present, a video of yourself presenting to adults. This may look daunting at first, but if you take it piece by piece, it can lead to a successful application, travel opportunities, and a chance to share your professional expertise.

The Bureau of Education Research (www.ber.org) in Bellevue, Washington, is the largest private company in the nation presenting one-day seminars for educators. Other bureaus include:

California Elementary Education Association   www.CEEA.org

TEC Professional Development   www.tec-coop.org

Speakers Guild, Inc.   www.speakersguild.com

National Speakers Association   www.nsaspeaker.org

Washington Speakers Bureau   www.washspkrs.com

Museums

Major museums have extensive education programs. There's a place for people who understand child development and learning strategies. Some have extensive teacher training programs and outreach effforts to schools. Your knowledge of school systems and the fundamentals of hands-on learning can pave the way to a position as a staff member, consultant, or trainer. Consult your local library or bookstore for museum directories, or log on to the following websites for lists of museums for kids:

Raisin: Children's Museums   www.raisinnet.com

Kid Zone   www.kidzone.com

American Youth Museums   www.aym.org

The Not-for-Profit World

The problem with the term "nonprofit" is that you immediately picture yourself living like Mahatma Ghandi. In fact, many not-for-profiteers earn husky salaries in luxurious surroundings. My first adventure in the NP world included a doorman, floor-to-ceiling windows on the seventeenth floor, cutting-edge technology, frequent travel, a generous per diem in some of my favorite cities, and a black marble restroom with fresh cut flowers every day. It took exactly one day to make the transition from my 1930s classroom to the lap of luxury.

There are full-service websites that can introduce you to not-for-profitting: directories of employers, job listings, career paths, government regulations, writing your own job description, negotiating salaries, and fringe benefits. Start with any of the following:

Opportunity NOCs   www.opportunitynocs.org
Chronicle of Philanthropy   www.philanthropy.com
Community Career Center   www.nonprofitjobs.org
Goodworks   www.goodworksonline.com
Nonprofit Career Center   www.nonprofitcareer.com
Nonprofit Times   www.nptimes.com
Idealist Nonprofit Jobs   www.idealist.org

Government Agencies Related to Education

The government is one of the largest nonprofit agencies in the country, and the subsection devoted to education could bring full employment to the population of a small state. Start online with the U. S. Department of Education or the National Center for Education Statistics.

Foundations and Institutes with an Educational Focus

Foundations and institutes are often the philanthropic offspring of an individual with a passion for excellence in education. They are another opportunity for a career change, since many of their positions require administrative experience, educational expertise, and a nose for politics and fund-raising. Start your Web investigation with the key words *education foundations*.

Author! Author!

Writing and consulting are two ways to translate your professional experience into a whole new career. There are dozens of publishers, Heinemann included, who prosper in the competitive publishing world by offering a list of new titles every season. They're constantly prospecting for new authors with fresh ideas, and they have staff trained to shepherd promising manuscripts to the finish line. They will gladly provide detailed guidelines for submitting your proposal, or you can consult your bookstore or library for how-to books full of excellent examples. If you know any published writers, ask for a copy of their proposals to use as models.

Writing a book is a long process. You need a good idea and the self-discipline to put in the seat-time. But there are few thrills greater than strolling into a bookstore in any major city and finding yourself on a shelf. Being in-print is a real door-opener for consulting, speaking, publishing periodical articles, and radio and television interviews.

Retooling

If it's been years since you revised your resume, you may be surprised to discover how much you've accomplished. But you'll never have that pleasure if you don't get started. The easiest way to generate a resume in short order is to hire someone. But you still have to collect all the dates, comb through your professional history, and then explain what all those titles mean to your resume writer. You could end up doing most of the work, and picking up the tab.

So if you're a do-it yourself-er, go to the library or go online. First stop: www.headhunter.net, which has lots of suggestions for making a career change, including the ten top resume mistakes. Here are some more steps to ease the process.

- If you decide to write a resume yourself, check your computer software for a resume feature. With one click, you can choose from a variety of auto-formats, and then concentrate on content.
- Make a list of every committee, commission, or task force on which you have served. Describe each in active, product-oriented language. For example: designed K–12 math assessment, created interactive science curriculum, analyzed achievement of minority students and recommended reforms to board, mentored new administrators, published guidelines for preschool start-up program, piloted electronic report cards.
- If you're applying for a similar position in the education community, you may want to clump your experience in categories such as:

    instructional leadership
    curriculum design
    policy and programs
    professional development

    articles and publications

    educational reform

    fellowships and institutes

    community service

- If you're applying for a job outside of the education community, analzye your activities and emphasize the skill aspect rather than the educational outcome. Use words like: *directed, trained, organized, produced, supervised, published.*

- Read the description of the job for which you are applying and use the same language in your resume and cover letter to draw a straight line between you and the job.

- Plan on revising or reshaping your resume every time you apply for a job. Tweaking a basic resume just takes a few minutes. Adding, highlighting, or deleting information can bring your job experience into sharp focus and catch the eye of your potential employer.

Moving Day

Whether you leave your school in a cloud of balloons, bound for the sweet green hills of retirement, or you quietly announce that you've chosen another way to spend your passion for education, departures can be truly bipolar experiences—so liberating that you can scarcely contain your delight, and at the same time, tinged with loss, and even bereavement. Be prepared. After all, it's not like you're walking out of IBM, or a high-rise office full of cubicles. You've been at the center of a learning community, and your enthusiasm for kids probably hasn't changed much since you were a brand-new teacher.

Take time to collect your thoughts, then compose a letter to staff and community. If you will also be announcing your departure at public meetings, make notes, as this can be very emotional. Be sure to thank your staff and community for the wonderful opportunity of leading the school; cite the strengths of the school and the work that you have accomplished together; express optimism for the future of the school. Keep your remarks brief and heartfelt.

Now you've taken care of the adults. Saying good-bye to students can take many forms. You can have a series of assemblies, walk from class to class, write a letter to all students, have an open-house in your office so students can drop by for a personal farewell, or just stand at the entrance and exits for a week and speak to as many kids as possible. These are the good-byes you'll remember for years and years to come.

Postscript

Suppose you choose gardening. You know from the start that it will be a challenge. It's grueling work that can scare you. It's risky business—passion always is—especially when played out in such a public forum, yet it's compelling in a way that leaves you with no choice but to forge ahead. That's the nature of life in the paradox-rich territory of ideas and feelings known as school.

Some days the best you can ask of yourself is to approach each task, each person, each child in a constructive, humane way, distilling a tiny drop of tolerance into every interaction, for above all, the principalship is a tool for social justice.

If you choose gardening, be generous with your power, but hold tenaciously to your vision. Be bold. Find the courage to make waves and the strength to protect the innovators. Recognize the certainty of distress. Hone your intellectual alertness, for your daily activities are intertwined with critical ethical issues. Nurture a sense of aesthetics—the garden is your magnum opus, giving pleasure to all who gaze upon it.

Know this. Deeply committed gardening will disrupt your life, and push you beyond yourself, to places you can't go on your own. Ultimately, it is an act of faith and love.

Choose gardening. I did—and I grew.

Bibliography

Adams, Douglas (1988). *The Long Dark Tea-Time of the Soul*. Madison: Turtleback Books.

———. 1980. *The Hitchhiker's Guide to the Galaxy*. New York: Harmony Books.

Barth, Roland. 1967. *The End of the Road*. New York: Doubleday.

Bernhard, Virginia. 1990. *A Durable Fire*. New York: Morrow.

Bryson, Bill (1998). *A Walk in the Woods*. New York: Broadway Books.

Dickens, Charles. 1844. *A Christmas Carol*. Philadelphia: Carey & Hart.

Dyer, Timothy. 1997. "Education's Crumbling Veneer of Civility." *NASSP News Leader* 45(3): 2, 20.

Graham, Katharine. 1997. *Personal History*. New York: Alfred Knopf.

Harris, Debra. 2000. *What Counts: How Forward-Thinking Leaders Recognize and Reward Employees*. Salt Lake City, UT: Franklin Covey.

King, Martin Luther Jr. 1986. *Stride Toward Freedom*. San Francisco: Harper Row.

Port, Lillian Lee. 1997. *A Survival Guide to Teacher Layyoffs*. Foster City, CA: California School Law Publishers.

———. 2000. *Between a Rock and a Hard Place: Law for School Administrators*. Foster City, CA: California School Law Publishers.

Silverstein, Shell. 1964. *The Giving Tree*. New York: Harper Row.

U. S. Department of Education and U. S. Department of Justice. (2000). Early Warning, Timely *Response: A Guide to Safe Schools*. Washington, D.C.: U. S. Printing Office.

Yorinks, Arthur. 1986. *Hey, Al*. New York: Farrar, Straus and Giroux.